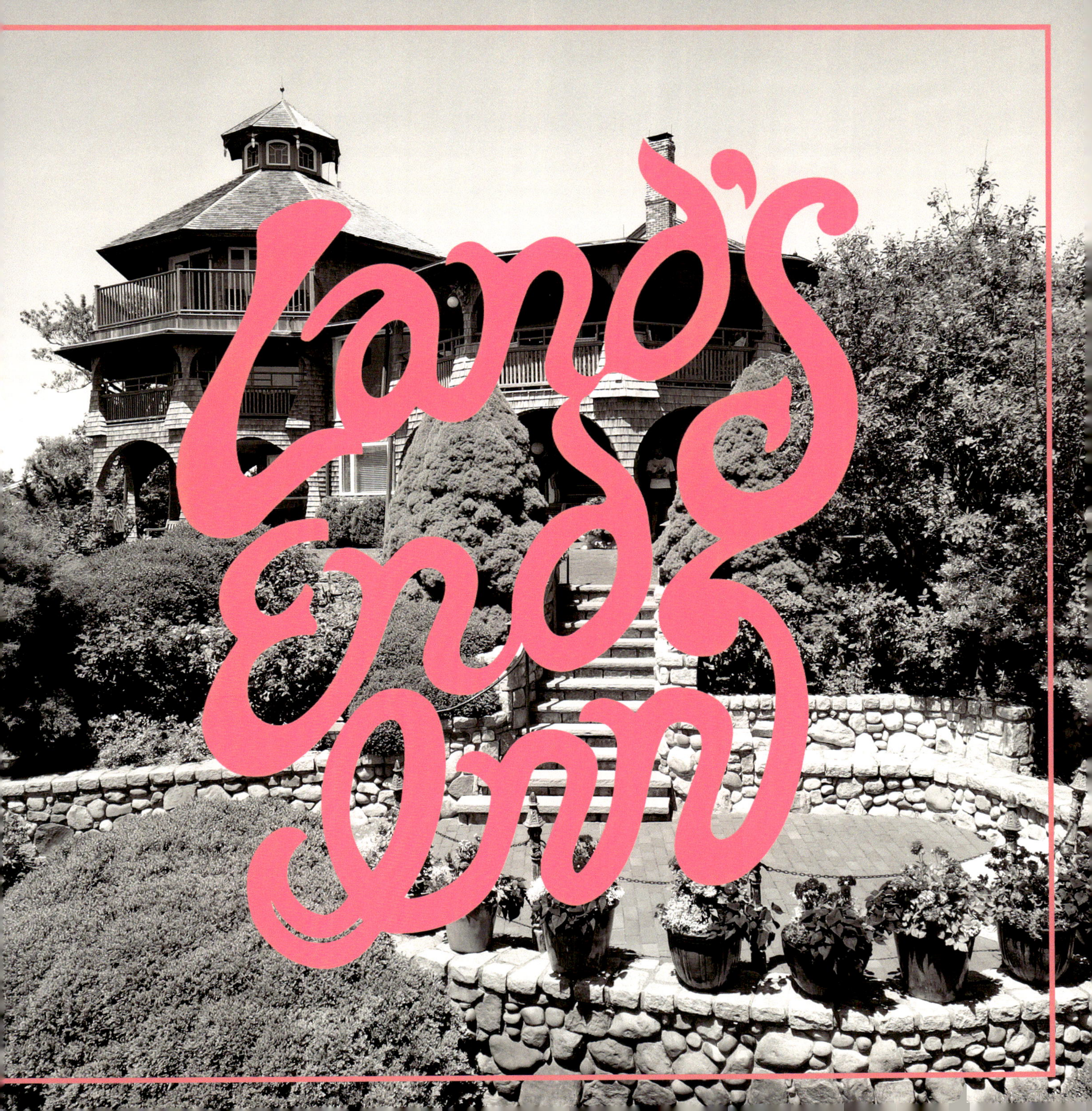
Land's
End
Inn

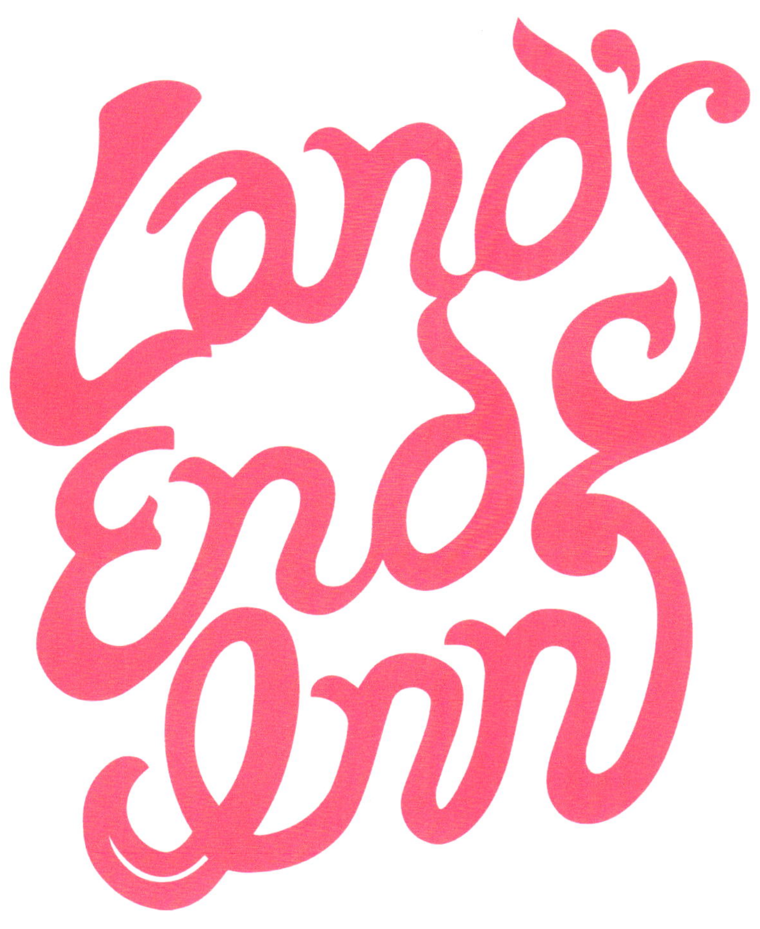

Ed Macri and Trevor Mikula

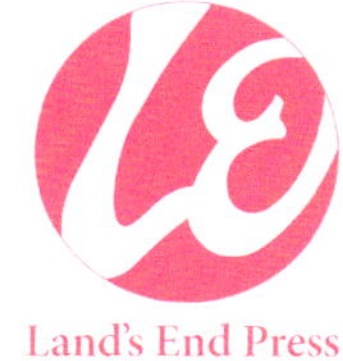

Land's End Press

Published by Land's End Press
Provincetown, MA
www.landsendinn.com

Photo credits. The following images are used with permission and are credited
to their respective owners:
Page 37: © Provincetown Magazine
Page 47: © Vincent Guadazno - USA TODAY NETWORK
Page 63: © Jim Gilbert - USA TODAY NETWORK
Pages 65, 71, 88: © Robert C. Cheney
Pages 66, 67, 68, 69, 70, 74, 75, 76, 77, 78, 79, 80: © Randall Perry
Page 83: © Coastal Engineering

Distributed by Greenleaf Book Group

For ordering information, please contact Greenleaf Book Group at PO Box 91869,
Austin, TX 78709, 512.891.6100.

Design, composition, and cover design by Land's End Press.

Publisher's Cataloging-in-Publication data is available.

Print ISBN: 979-8-9908469-0-6

To offset the number of trees consumed in the printing of our books, Greenleaf
donates a portion of the proceeds from each printing to the Arbor Day Foundation.
Greenleaf Book Group has replaced over 50,000 trees since 2007.

Printed in the United States of America on acid-free paper

24 25 26 27 28 29 30 31   10 9 8 7 6 5 4 3 2 1

First Edition

Contents

Preface

This book is the collective work of all the people who have owned and shepherded Land's End Inn over the last 120 years. We—Ed Macri and Trevor Mikula—are the current owners. When we had the good fortune to purchase the inn in 2022, we found a "fun" closet tucked away off the lobby. In it, among an array of martini shakers, candles, an original china set from 1904, and other sundries, we found two bankers boxes full of archives. These archives included postcards of original photos of the inn's interior, news articles interviewing prior owners sharing their musings about the inn, a treasure trove of photos, and, most importantly, three separate work-in-progress manuscripts telling the story of the inn. Those manuscripts, each annotated heavily with photos and commentary about the inn, were the fodder for this book. It is a magical place, and that was not lost on any of its shepherds. Each owner wanted to tell this story, and we are honored to present that to you in this book.

Trevor is an artist—a painter—who has anchored his lifelong career with a singular mission to make people happy. His unmistakable style of painting inspires conversations with its sophisticated, colorful, and unexpected compositions of everything from stunning florals to the kitchen sink. He is self-taught and paints with a vivid imagination, vibrant paint, and a palette knife. He has an avid following of collectors, and his work shows in galleries across the country. Ed DJs as "Lazerella" at local clubs, including the legendary A-House, and previously had a career in technology, including fourteen years as an executive at Wayfair.

Ed first came to Provincetown in 1993 for a long weekend and returned each year for all its magic until it ultimately became home. Trevor first visited Provincetown in 2012 on the recommendation of some good friends who thought that this was where he belonged. He moved here a few months later and opened an art gallery. Although we knew each other during those years, we came together in 2019, nine months after the untimely death of Ed's prior partner, Will Rowan. We married the following year. Provincetown brought us together. Its community has provided Trevor with incredible inspiration for his art. For Ed, it provided support and the biggest imaginable group hug after Will's death.

Before we bought the inn, we had no experience in hospitality and no specific aim to buy an inn. We did have a deep love for Provincetown—a town whose community had already given us so much—and a latent desire to give something back and help preserve its landmarks for generations to come. Unbeknownst to us, we were setting ourselves on a course to do exactly that when we purchased the house next to the inn in 2020. Our house is where we married that summer and, among other things, Trevor wanted to create a sculpture garden. That plan ultimately included a memorial garden for Will. Seeing the vision come together, we began to wonder about who might buy it after our deaths and whether the sculptures would continue to be enjoyed and cherished. We found inspiration during a walk through Suzanne's Garden, a lovely plot of land in Provincetown's East End that is designated as a public garden for the enjoyment of all. That quickly became the long-term vision for our home too.

As new neighbors, we got to know Stan and Eva Sikorski, the owners of Land's End Inn at the time. We learned from them that the gardener of the inn in the 1940s, Wally O'Donnell, built the home we had just purchased. Velma O'Donnell, Wally's wife, sold us the house after living there for more than seventy years. The connections were subtly lining up, and the universe was taking us in a direction we had never imagined. Stan and Eva presented the opportunity to purchase the inn with the understanding that we would preserve and evolve its place in the community. When a door like that opens, you say yes and step in. It might be scary, and it will surely evolve differently than you imagined, but you move ahead because the only regret would be not stepping in.

As we explored the boxes of archives we found in the fun closet, we pleasantly discovered kindred spirits in the prior owners—particularly Charles Higgins, who built the inn in 1904, and David Schoolman, who owned it from 1972 to 1995, when he died of AIDS. Charles built a quirky, artistic bungalow improbably at the top of a sand dune at the remotest point on Cape Cod, and brought the local arts community together there. David preserved all of its quirkiness, added two towers and a veranda, expanded the decks, and threw a lot of fun parties along the way. A love of art (and artists), a call to build what one can dream, and a desire to bring people together fueled the inspirational energy behind their work and ours.

Enjoy this history of Land's End Inn. Most importantly, visit us and experience it in person, whether for an overnight stay, a glass of wine on the lawn, or a stroll around the grounds. Drink in the view!

Ed & Trevor

Way Up Along... Where the Land Ends

Land's End Inn sits atop Gull Hill, the highest point at the end of the glacial spiral of land that is Cape Cod. It was originally the summer home of Charles Lothrop Higgins, who built the house in 1904. After Charles's death in 1926, the house was sold and opened as an inn and teahouse. It has operated as an inn ever since.

The property known as Gull Hill is first mentioned in the last will and testament of Captain Jonathan Nickerson, a member of a prominent fishing family at the time. The hill, surrounding pastures, and seaside property were all assessed at $300 in his 1871 will.

Charles purchased Gull Hill, now known as 22 Commercial Street, in September 1903. The property stretched over three acres and included some waterfront property across Commercial Street. Houses dating from around 1800 and others which had been floated over from Long Point circa 1860 already lined Commercial Street. Locals then called this part of Provincetown's West End "Way Up Along." Here, one was indeed at "land's end" because the road terminated at the Red Inn, where there was a turnaround and a town landing. Beyond were tidal flats, marshes, and grass farms.

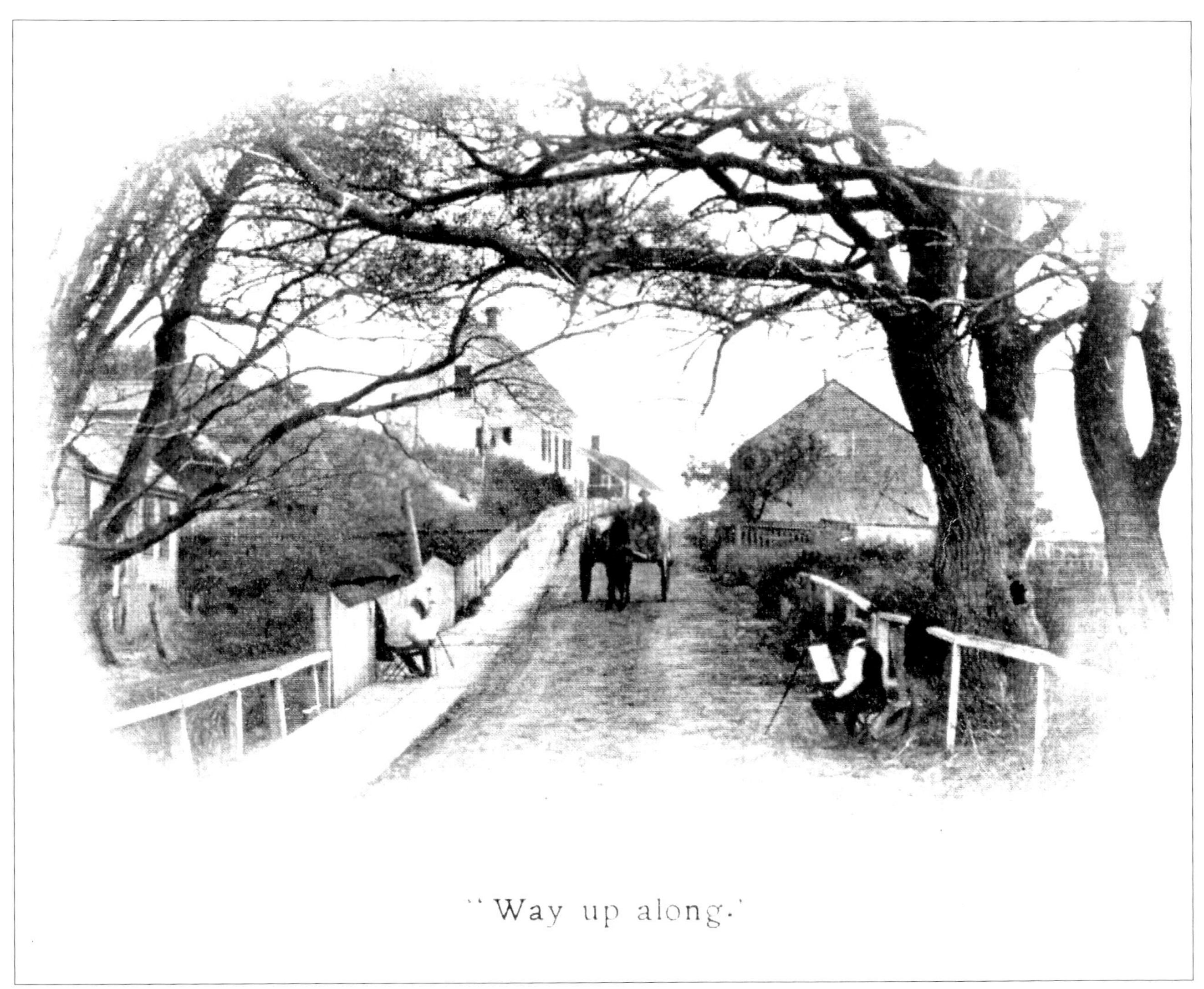

Looking east up Commercial Street from the Red Inn, circa 1900

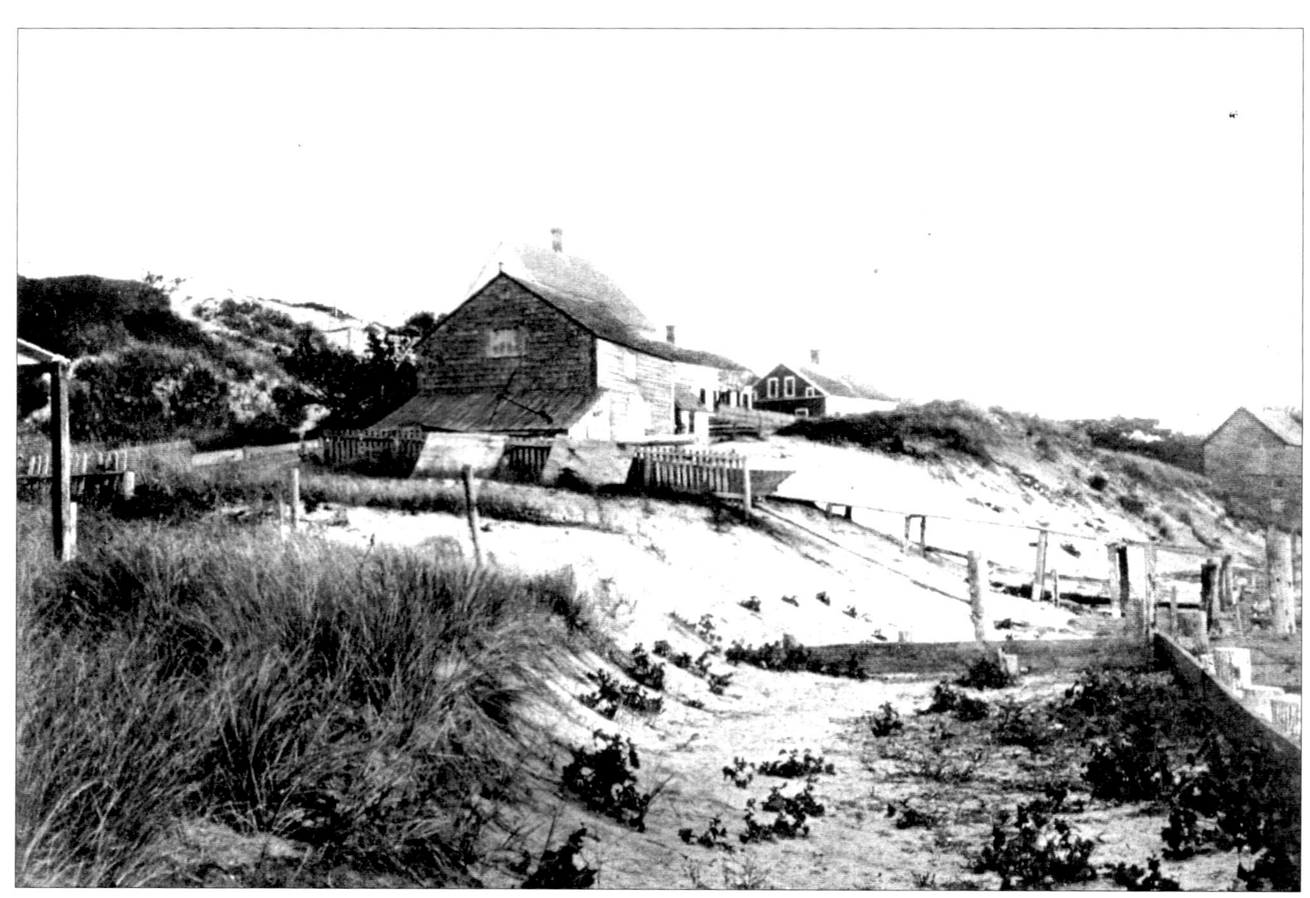

Looking up from the beach at the present entrance to Land's End Inn at the foot of Gull Hill, circa 1900

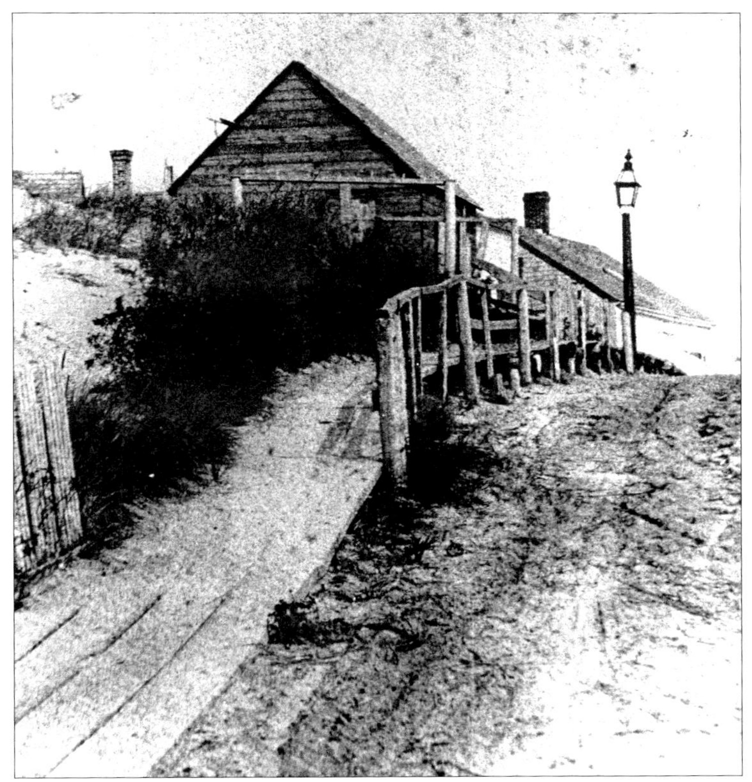

Looking east up Commercial Street at the present entrance to Land's End Inn, circa 1900. The roof with the chimney on the right is 26 Commercial Street.

Higgins's Bungalow... Built in 1904

Charles Lothrop Higgins was born in Provincetown on April 9, 1863, the son of two very old Cape Cod families. His father, Isaac Henry Higgins, was a descendant of Richard Higgins, one of the first Nauset settlers in 1644. His mother, Harriet Nye White, could trace her ancestry back to Peregrine White, who was the first baby boy born on the Pilgrim ship *Mayflower* in the harbor of Cape Cod in 1620. Isaac Higgins was a shipbuilder. Soon after the demise of the salt and fish industries in Provincetown, he moved his family to Gloucester, Massachusetts, where Isaac continued his work.

Although Charles was raised in Gloucester, he studied in the West Indies. He was a world traveler and well-known lecturer. He lived in the fashionable sections of Boston's Beacon Hill and Back Bay, drove a Liberty car, and belonged to the city's oldest and most prestigious fraternity, the Masonic Saint John's Lodge. He worked as a haberdasher on Boston's Newbury Street. Never married, he built a summer home at Gull Hill in 1904 and lived there as a "single gentleman." Friend to many in the arts and theater, Charles began the inn's history of supporting Provincetown's arts community.

Charles built a landmark. The site placement he chose was remarkable. Defying convention at the time, he set the residence far back from and high above the road. The tedious climb for all who visited remained until the 1950s, when the owners paved a drive to the backside of the house from Point Street. The architecture was quirky and dramatic. A giant picture window framed commanding views of Provincetown Harbor and beyond, and a playful octagon housed the primary bedchamber and office. Built on stilts to add elevation—an early version of air conditioning—the house had porches that imitated the decks of a ship and afforded views from every side. Inside the house, windows rolled up and down into the woodwork to assist with cross-ventilation. There were two faucets of running water. Artistic finishes by local craftspeople filled the interior with warmth and character. Like so much of the original artisanal work, the stained glass and the art nouveau chandelier that crowned its Great Room in 1904 can still be seen in place, preserved to this day.

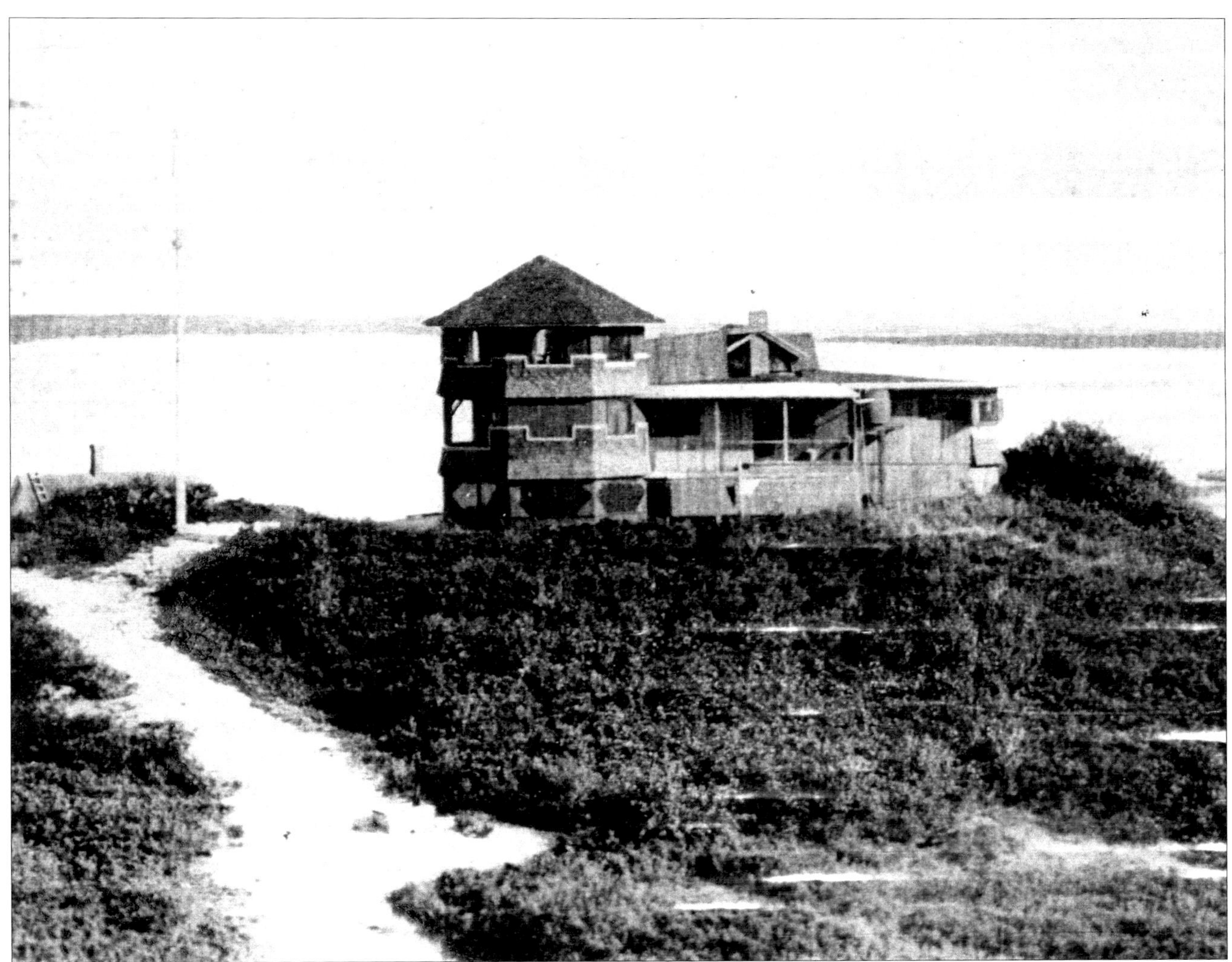

Higgins's bungalow on Gull Hill, circa 1910

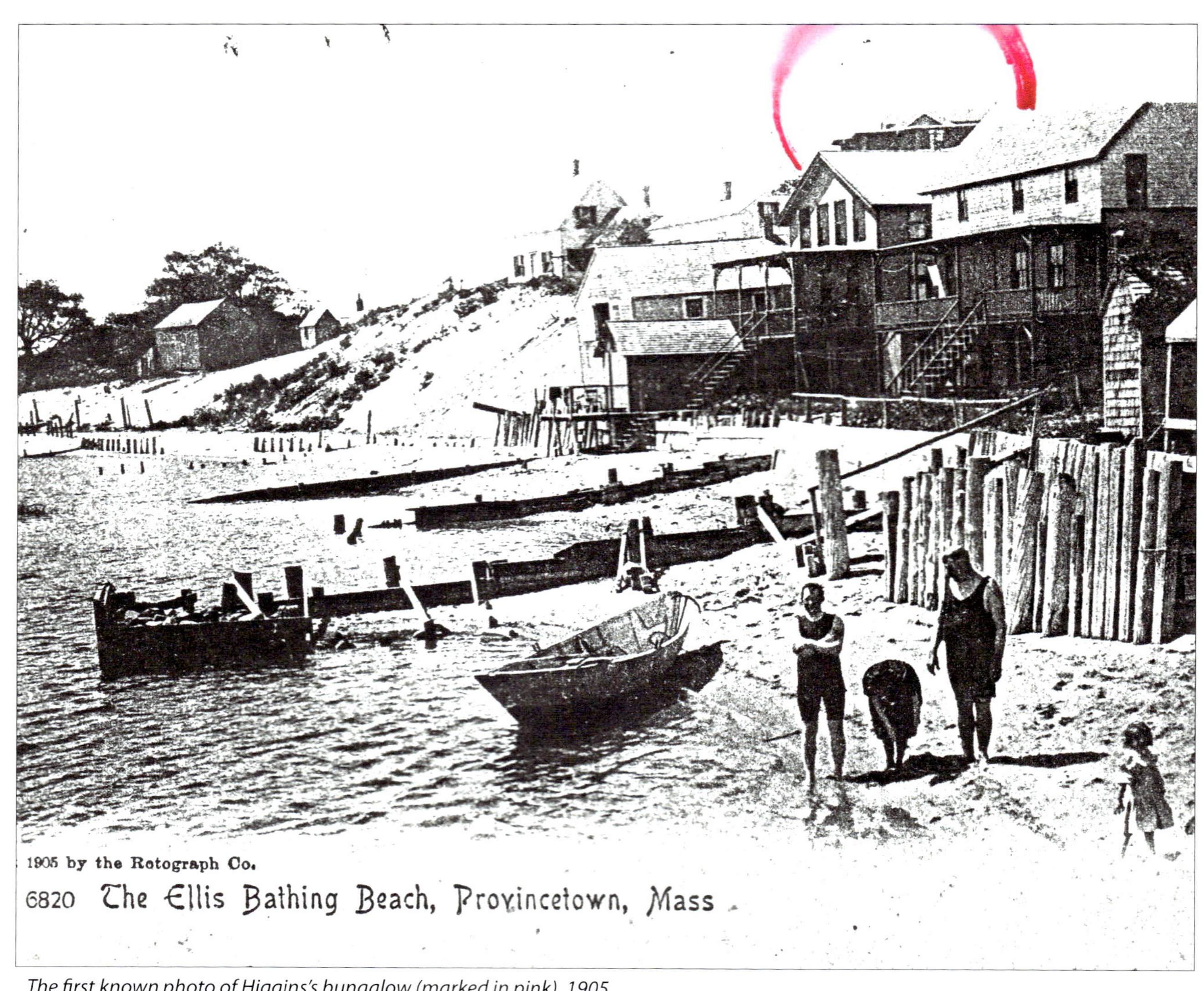

The first known photo of Higgins's bungalow (marked in pink), 1905

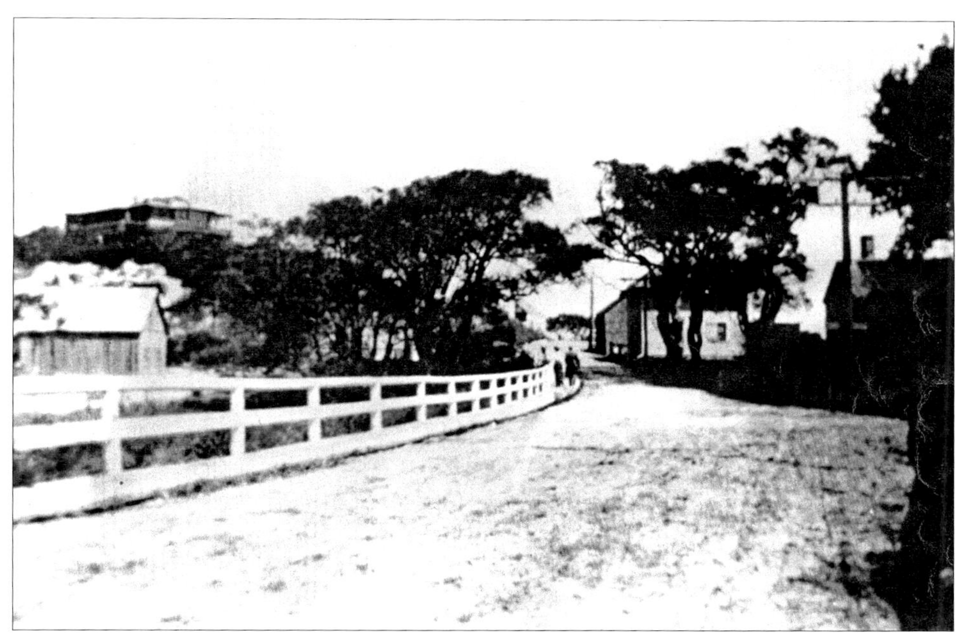

Looking east up Commercial Street toward Higgins's bungalow from the Red Inn, circa 1910

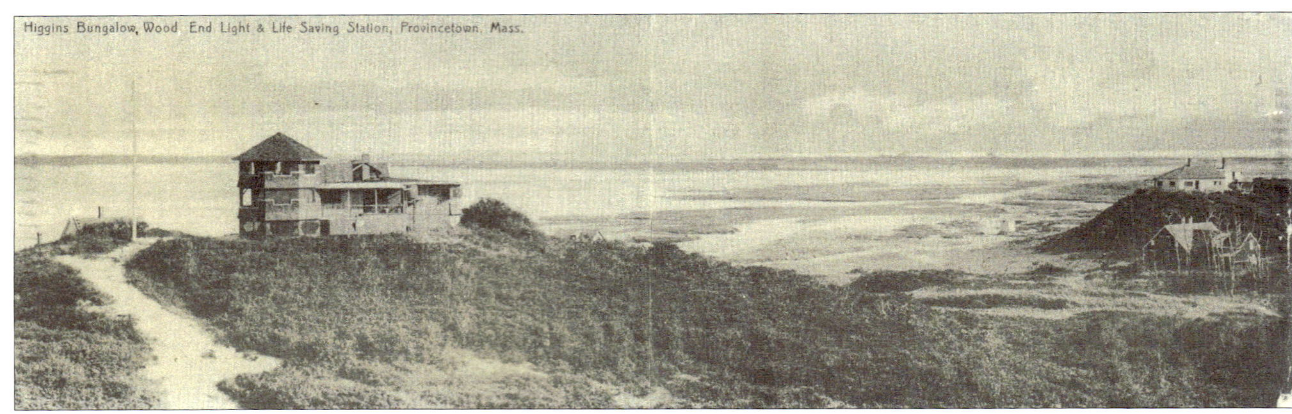

A postcard of the bungalow, which Higgins printed, circa 1910

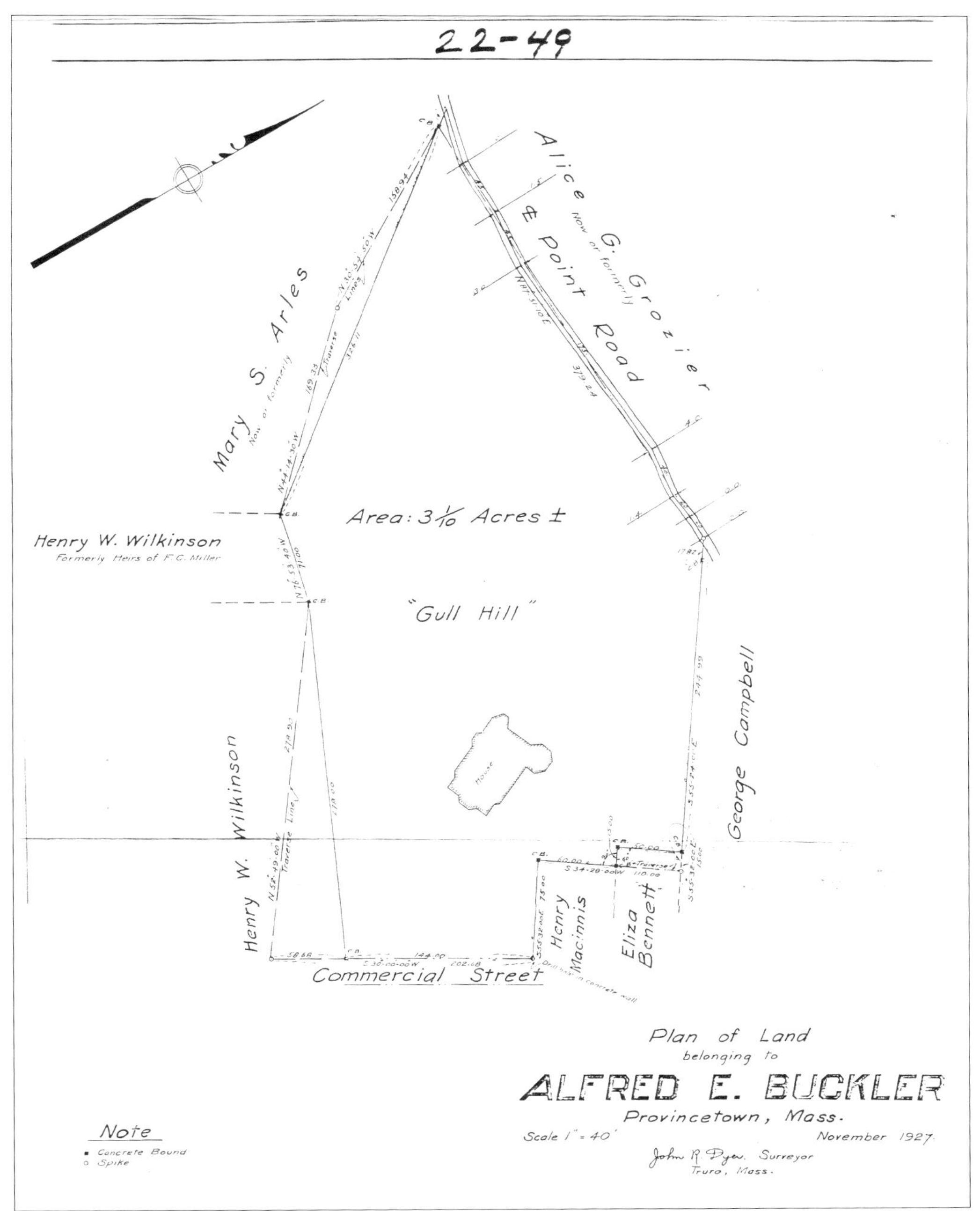

First recorded plan of land, 1927

17

WHILE I WAS MUSING THE FIRE BURNED

- Engraving on fireplace mantel

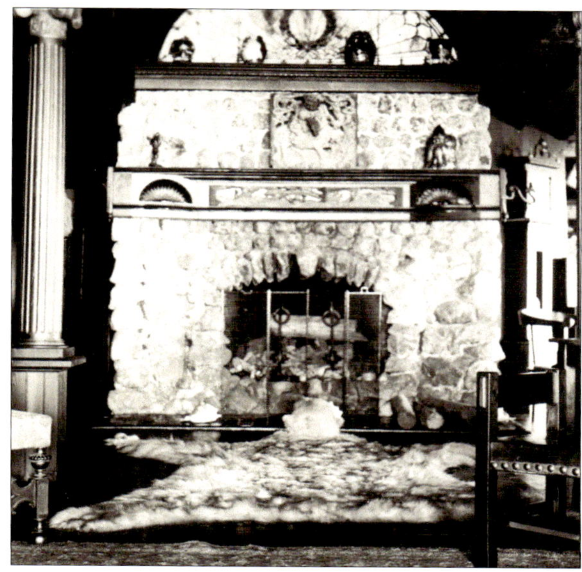

Great Room adorned with stonework and woodwork by local artisans, circa 1910

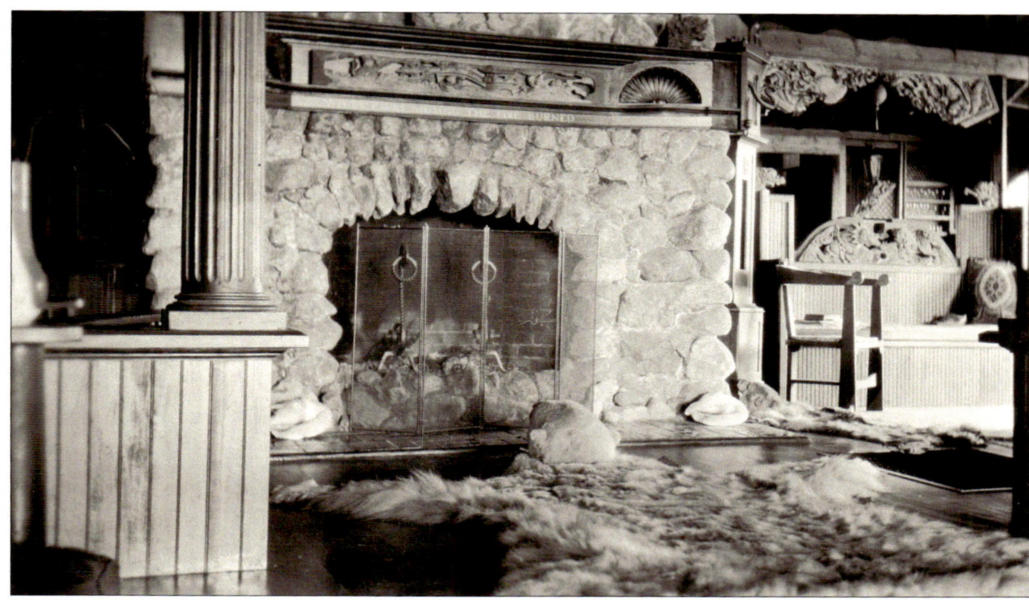

Great Room, circa 1910. The fireplace, the stained glass above it, the grandfather clock to the left, and the columns remain unchanged to this day.

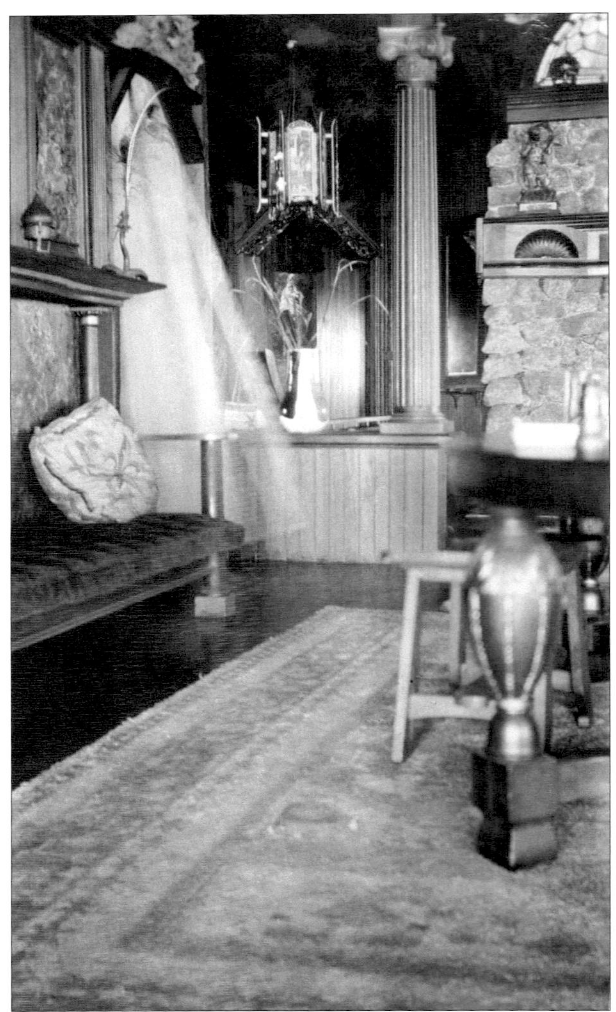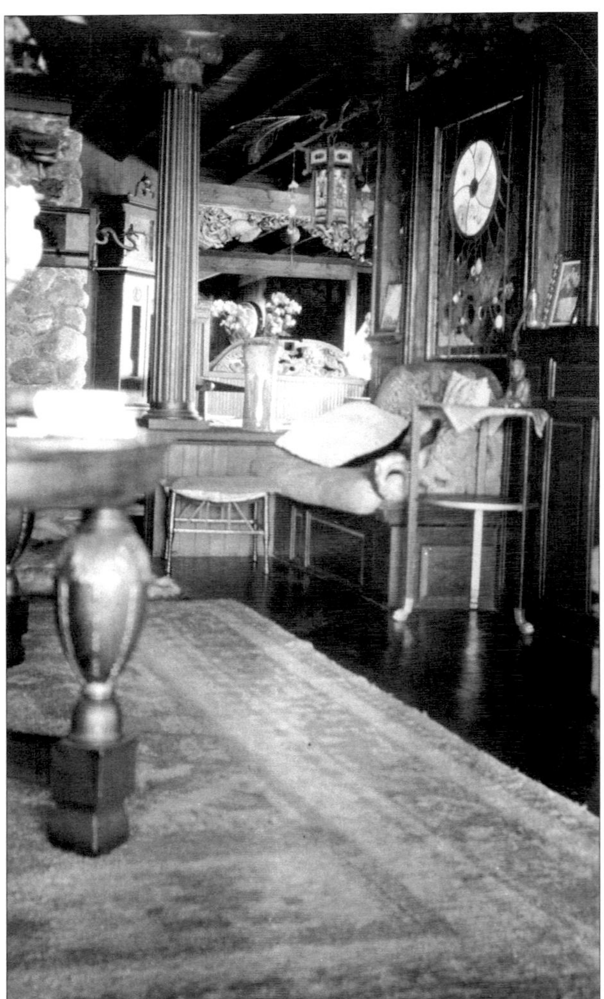

Great Room, circa 1910

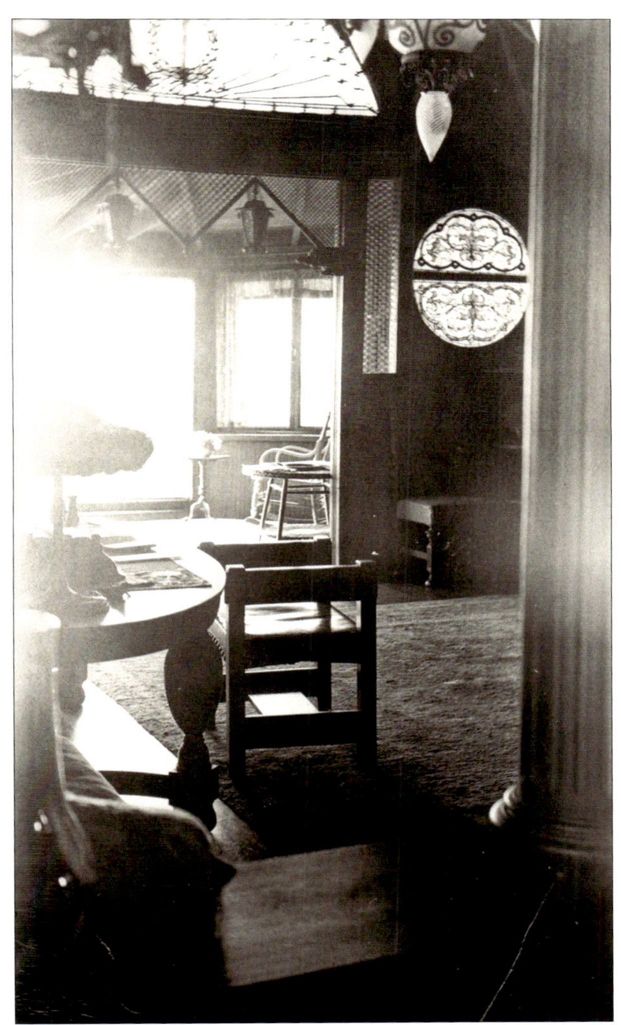

Looking toward the Solarium from the Great Room, circa 1910. The stained glass and Great Room chandelier remain in place today.

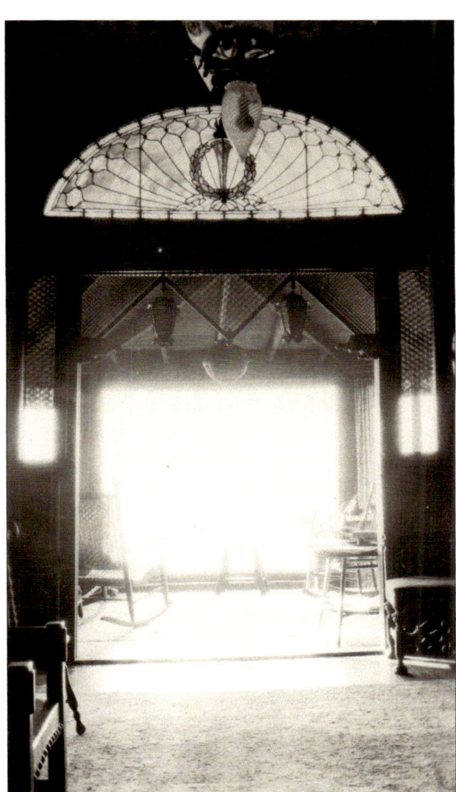

Solarium, circa 1910

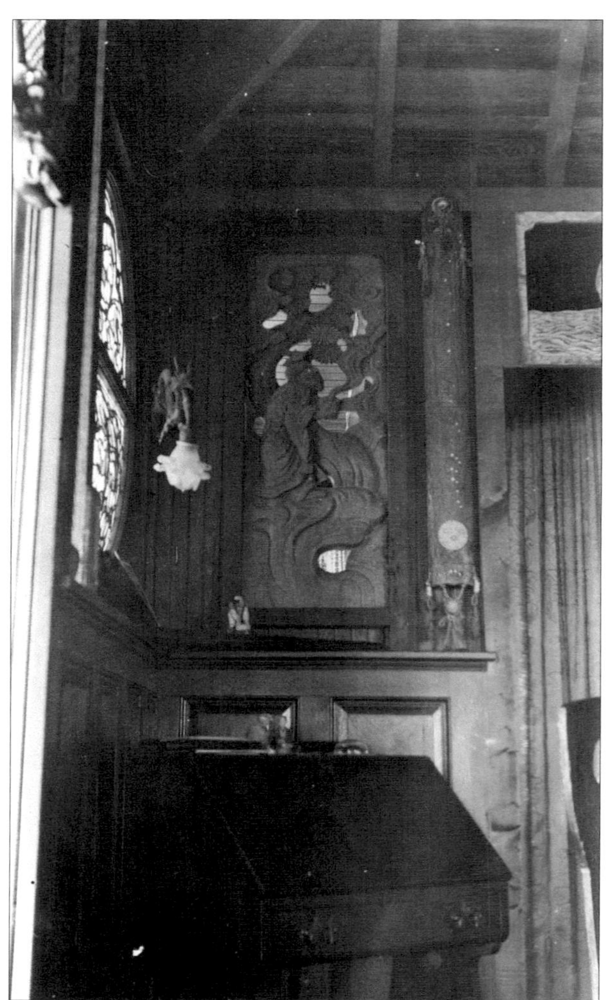

Wood carvings in the walls of the Great Room, circa 1910

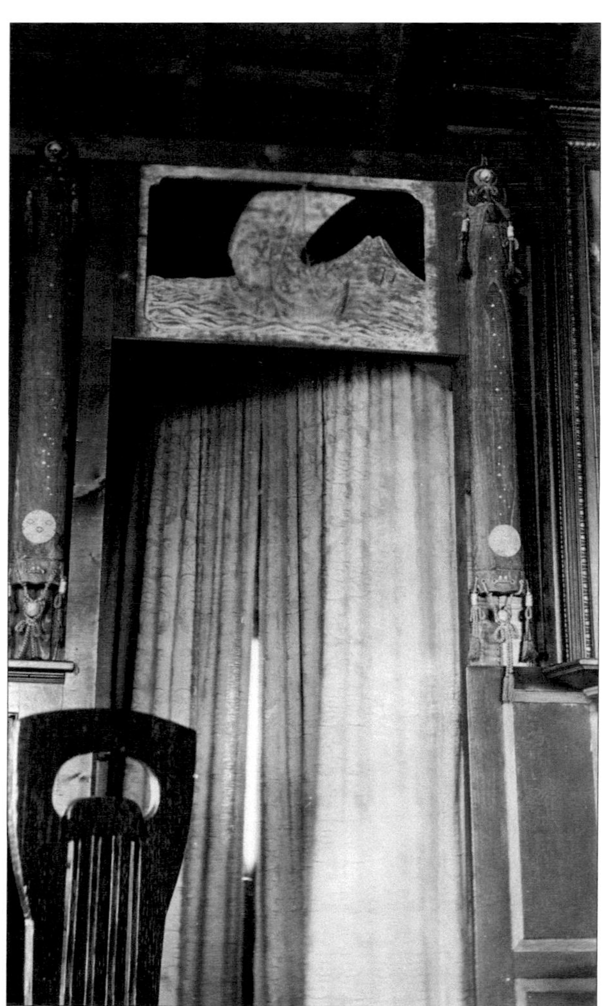

Doorway to today's Library and Gold Rooms, circa 1910

One hundred twenty years later, the quirky, quintessential Provincetown spirit of the bungalow remains alive, preserved physically in details throughout the house, including woodwork, stonework, and stained glass, and spiritually through its magical allure, which draws people in and brings them together.

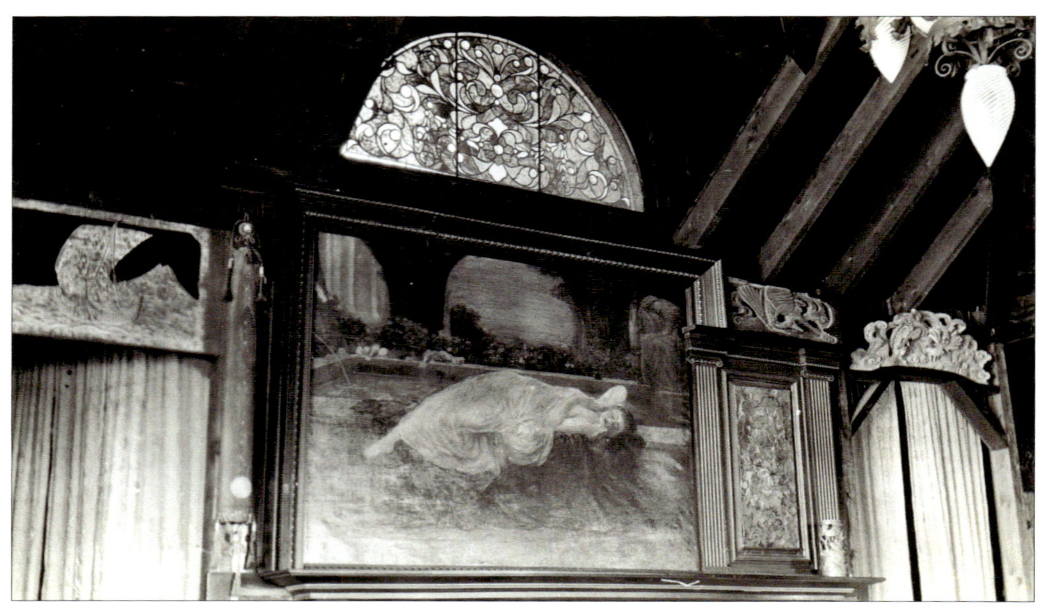

Eastern wall of the Great Room, circa 1910

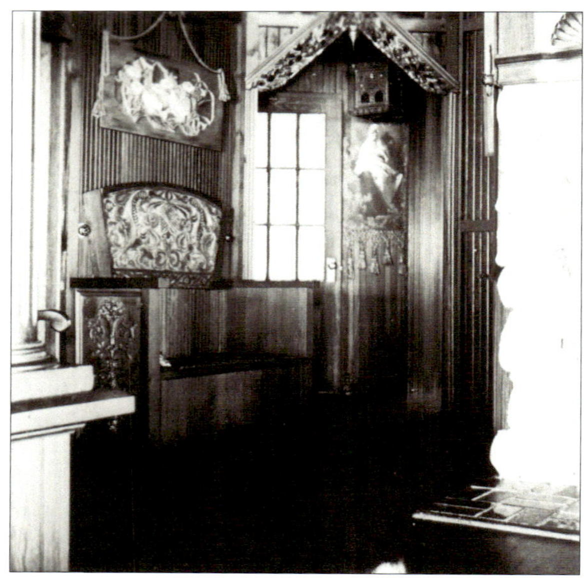

Nook by today's Tiger Lily and Victorian Rooms, circa 1910

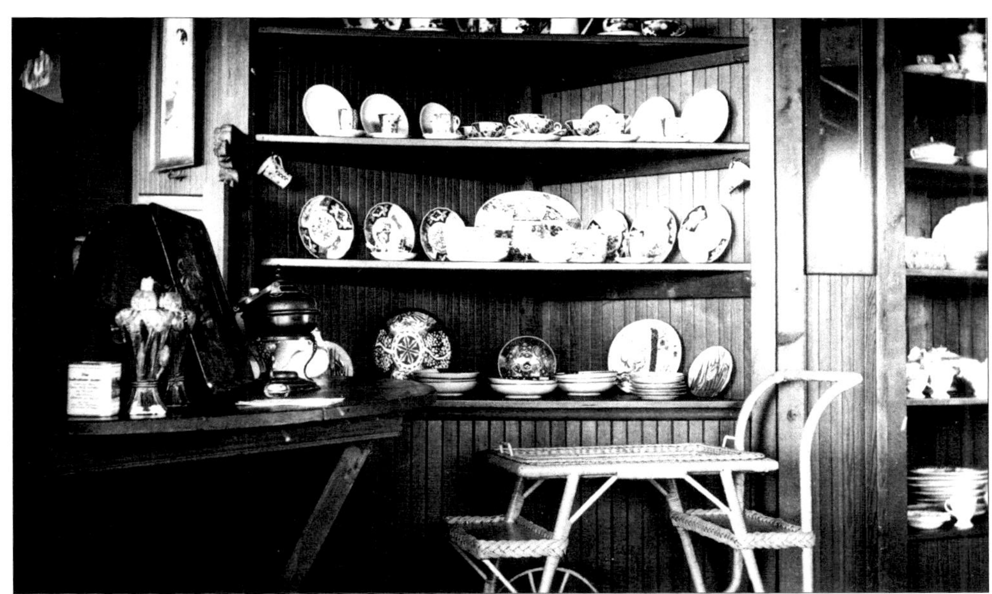

Open china cabinet behind today's front desk, circa 1910

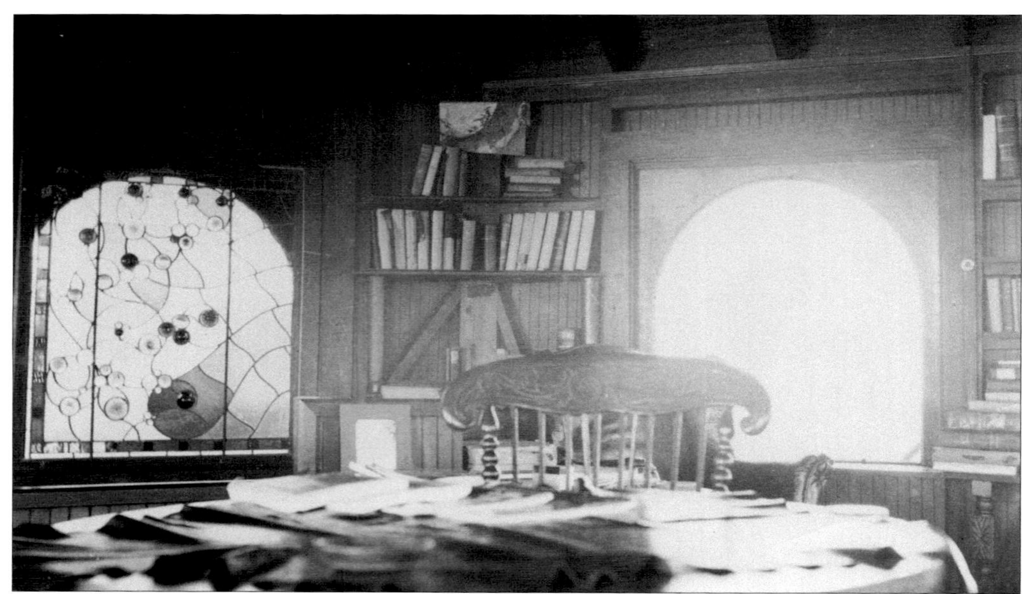

Higgins's office in what is now the Moroccan Tower Room, circa 1910

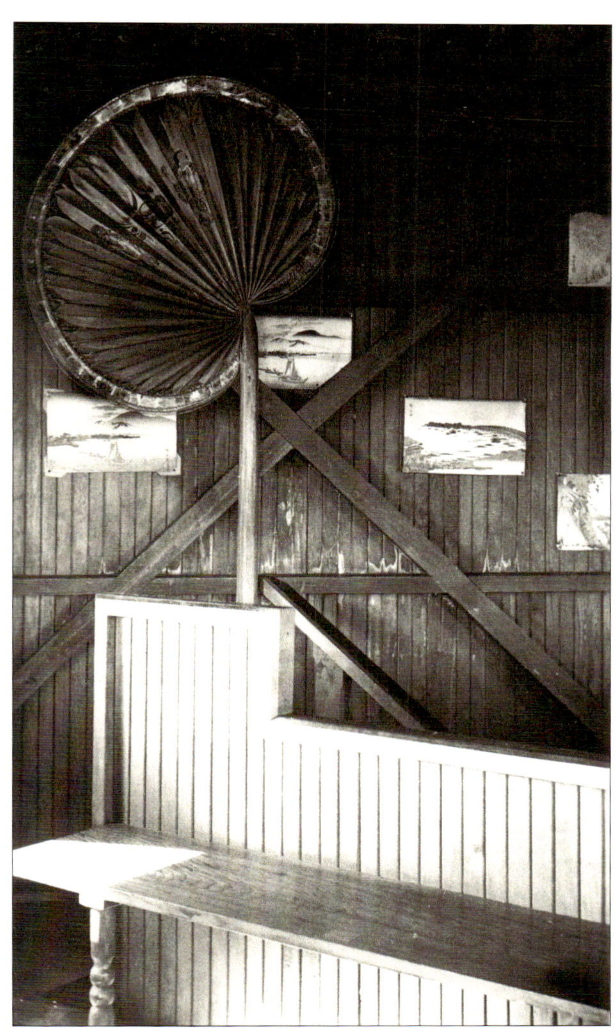

Stair rail coming into Higgins's office, circa 1910

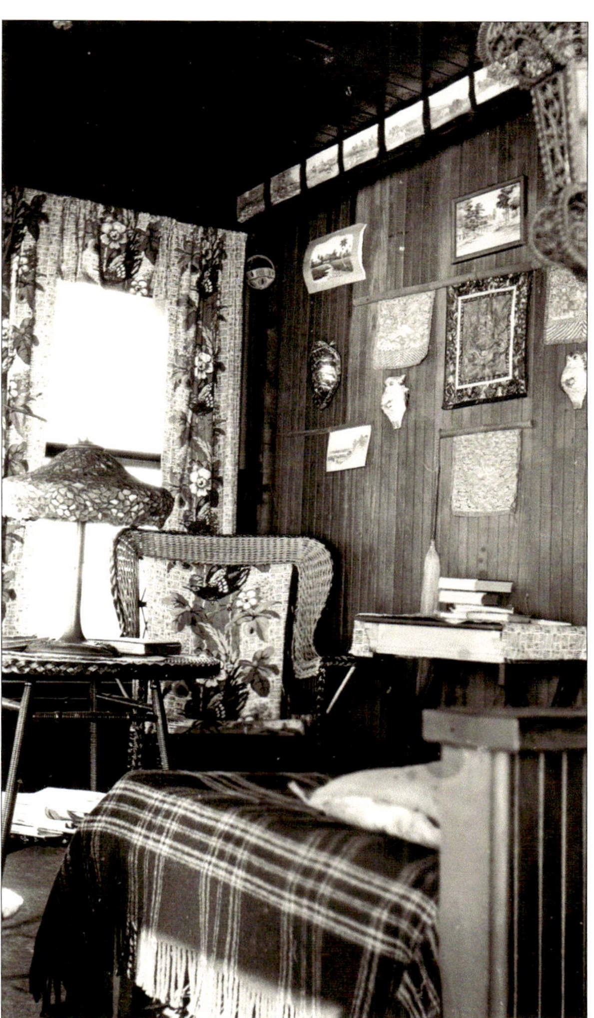

*Bedroom (exact location in house unknown), circa 1910.
Then, as now, every room was filled with treasures.*

Tea Room... Open to the Public

After Charles Higgins's death in 1926, the Buckler family purchased his bungalow. The Bucklers were from Providence, Rhode Island, and they owned a summer cottage across from the bungalow. After acquiring the property, they offered rooms for rent and opened a Russian tea room. From then on, the property became known as Land's End Inn. The Bucklers were avid travelers and brought back artifacts from around the world, many of which are on display in the inn today.

In the 1930s, then-gardener Wally O'Donnell removed sand from around the lower level to allow the addition of garden-level rooms. He used the sand to develop the flat area northeast of the inn. When Wally married in 1951, the Bucklers gave him that land as a wedding gift and thank-you for years of hard labor. Wally built a kit house on the property for his wife, Velma. Wally died in 2010 at the age of ninety-seven. Velma lived there until the age of ninety-two, when she sold the property to us.

The Bucklers owned the inn until 1955, when they sold it to Norman Lague and his stepbrother, Jules Wade. Their association with the house began with Norman's great aunt, Madame Cyr, a milliner in Danielson, Connecticut. She and hatter Charles Higgins had become acquainted, and she would bring her great nephews, Norman and Jules, to Higgins's bungalow. They continued to visit the house after it passed to the Buckler family and before they later purchased it from the Bucklers.

Because of health complications, Jules visited the inn only occasionally. But Norman made it his home and gained renown in the local arts community as an editor, writer, pianist, composer, actor, dramatist, artist, and craftsman. He was a mainstay of the Provincetown Theater Workshop and one of its governors. Although few photos exist from this time, they had a grand piano in the living room. At some point, they replaced the quintessential Cape Cod wood shingles on the exterior with white vinyl siding.

The Bucklers, Norman Lague, and Jules Wade cemented three important traditions that carry on to this day. The first is that Higgins's bungalow is open to the public as an inn. The second is that all its furnishings pass from owner to owner, gifting us today with remarkable treasures going back as many as 120 years, to Higgins's time. And the third is that the inn maintains strong ties to and supports the local arts community.

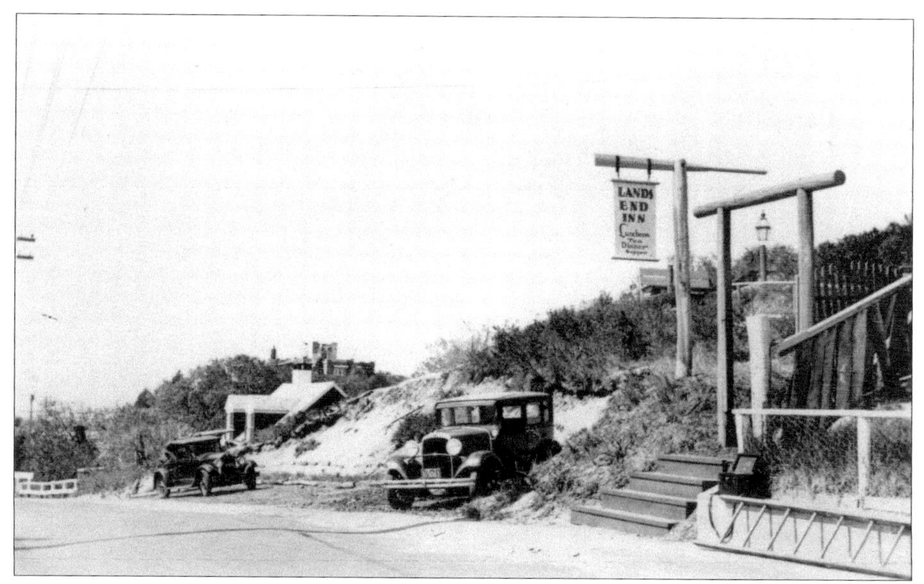

Entrance to Land's End Inn from Commercial Street, circa 1930

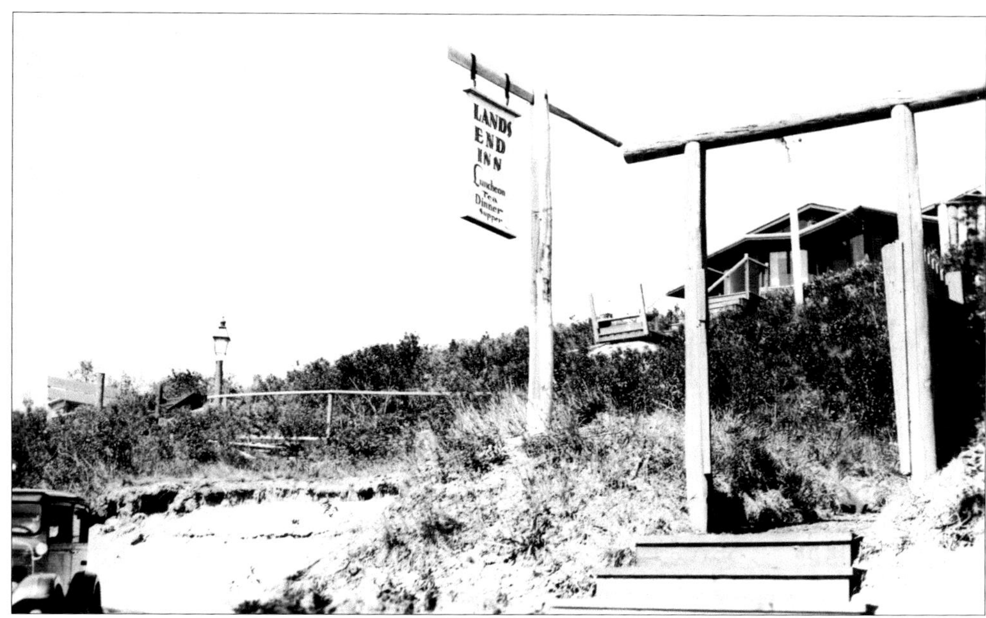

First Land's End Inn sign welcoming the public, circa 1930

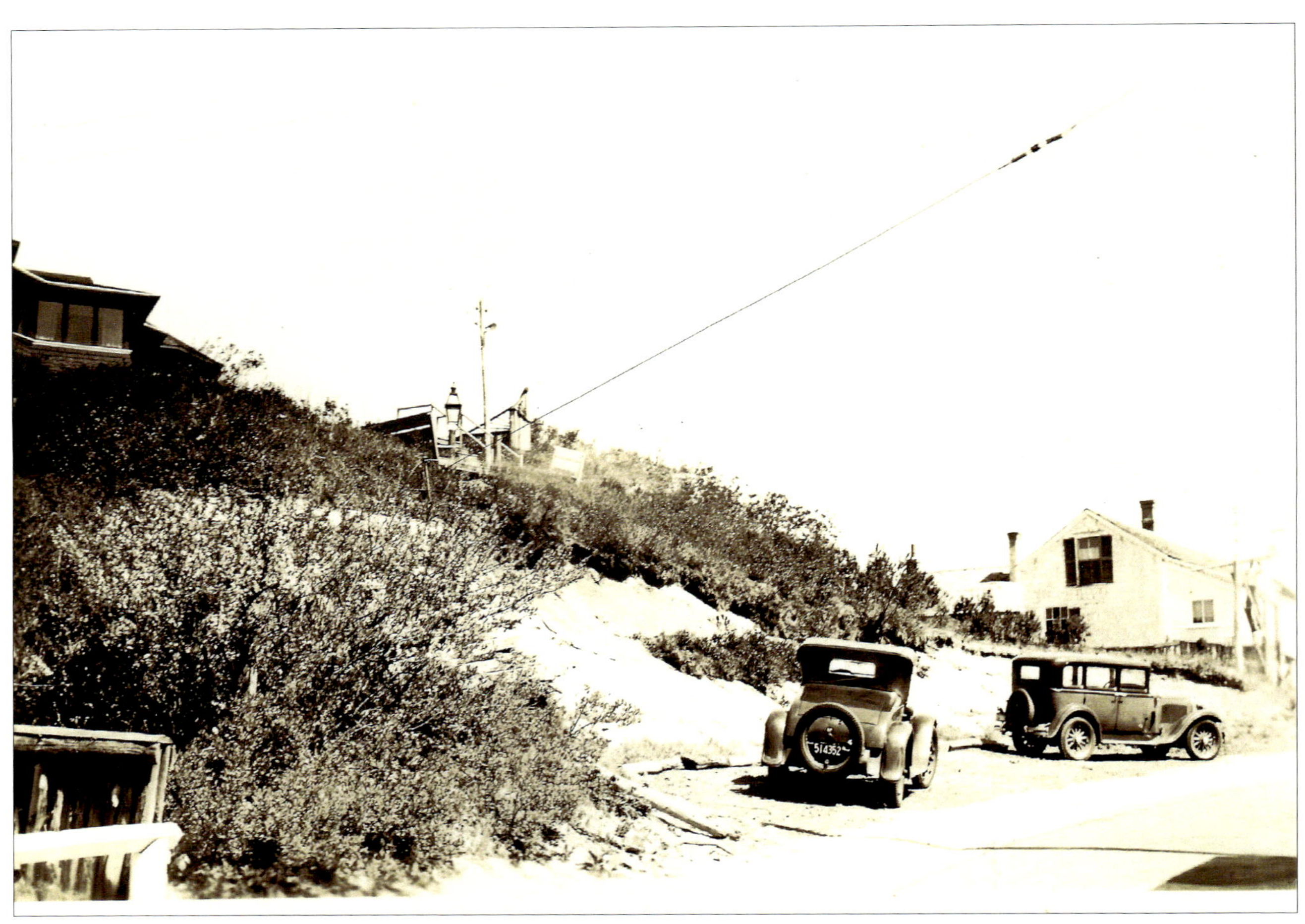

Parking in front of Land's End Inn along Commercial Street, circa 1930

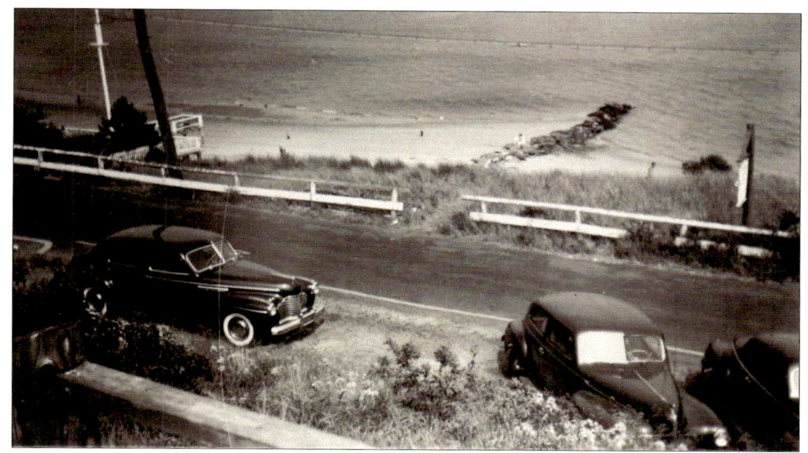

Beach across Commercial Street from Land's End Inn, circa 1930

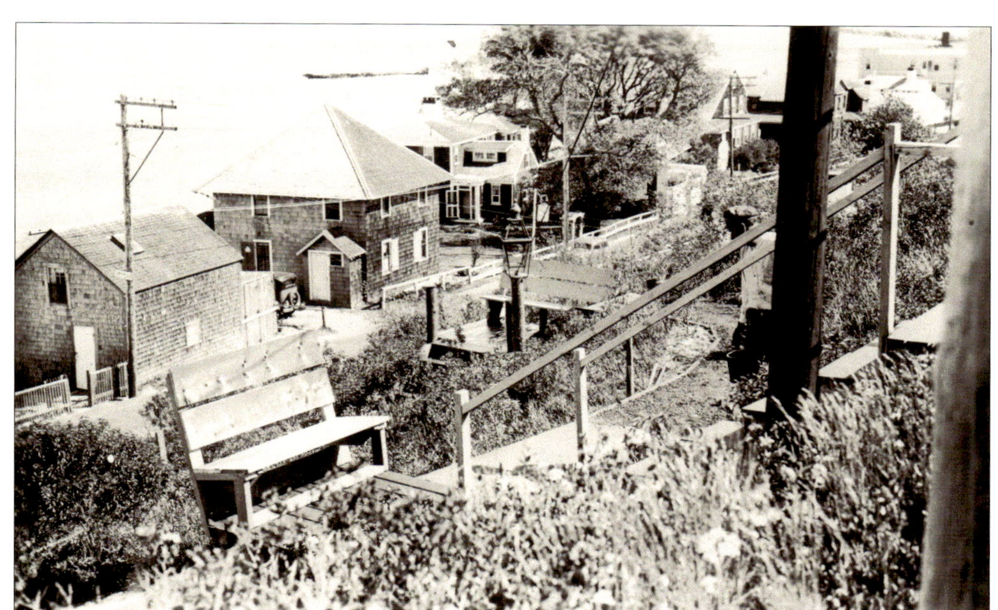

Looking down from Land's End Inn at summer cottages and the Red Inn along Commercial Street, circa 1930

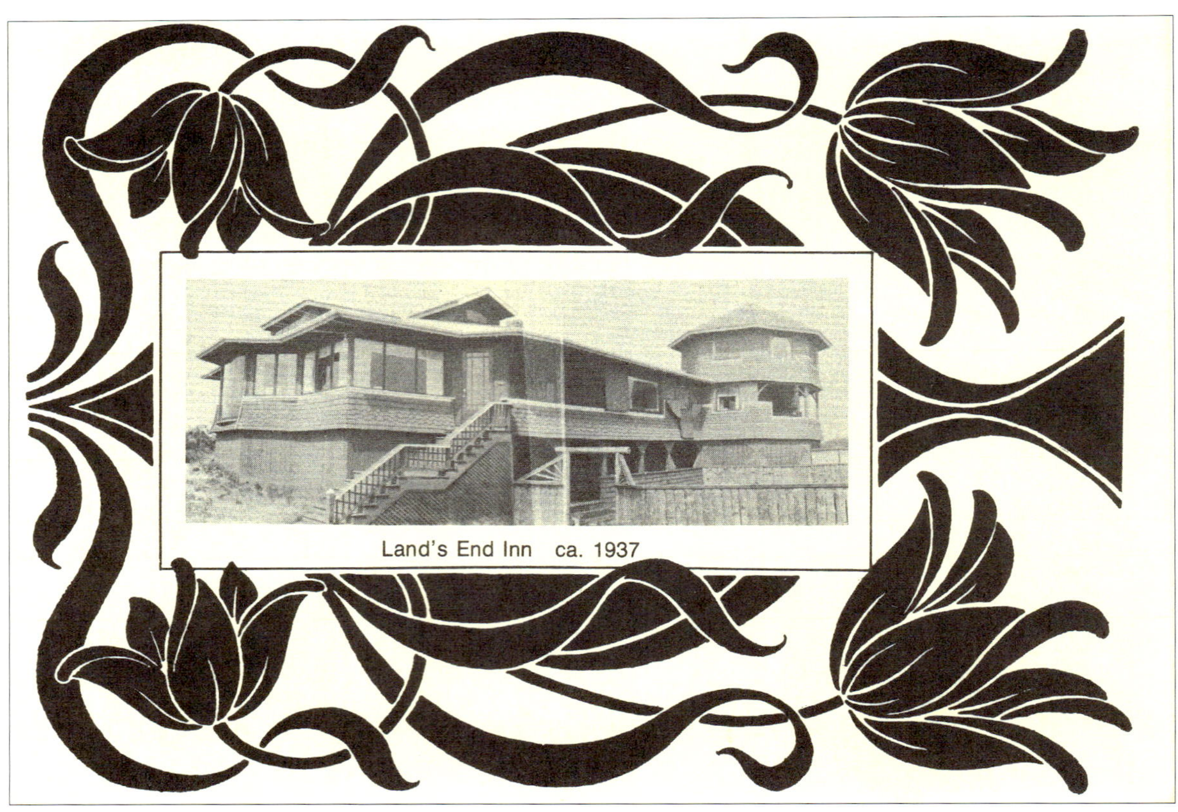

Postcard, circa 1960, depicting Land's End Inn, circa 1937

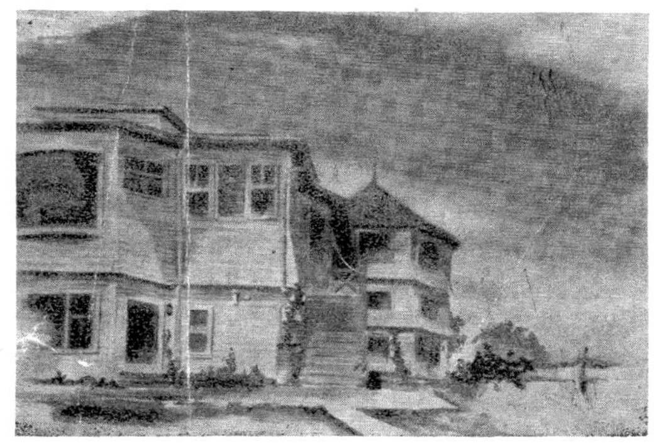

Norman and Jules invite you to share the hospitality of

land's end inn

on Gull Hill, Provincetown, Mass., at the very end of Cape Cod

which commands a panoramic view of Cape Cod Bay, Provincetown, its harbor, and its picturesque, finger-like wharfs.

We are within a comfortable walking distance to the center of town, excellent restaurants, sandwich bars, unique gift and handicraft shops, art galleries, and portrait artists.

Sandy beaches are nearby, we have our own private beach, and the quiet waters of the bay entice the swimmer, or those who prefer just plain day-dreaming.

Our inn, originally Captain J. Higgins' summer home, was built well over a hundred years ago. Comfortable and

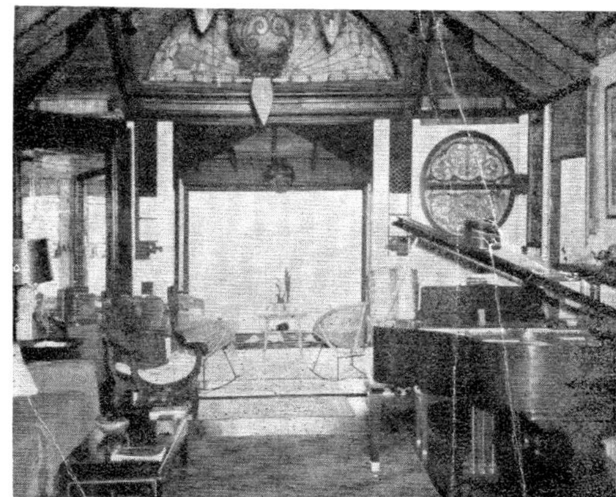

(Living room, looking out to the curved, Italian Glass Window)

pleasant innovations have been made to the structure, without changing its unique, old-world charm.

We have preserved the Teak wood carvings, old Tiffany Glass Windows, Venetian Glass Chandelier and the hand-wrought Italian lanterns. We have also added many of our own treasures from those "far away places".

For those of you who are active, Provincetown is a vacationer's paradise—hiking or jeep buggying over the dunes—horseback riding — leisurely sightseeing flights over the Cape's tip in a Piper Cub — sailing — fishing — skin diving — golf — tennis — swimming in bay or ocean — fresh-water swimming — interesting off-beaten Cape lanes to explore — OR, if you insist on wearing those "spectator pumps" — there is the theatre — playhouse — or just "settin" on our patio.

Brochure (notably exaggerating the age of the inn and Higgins's status as a captain), circa 1960

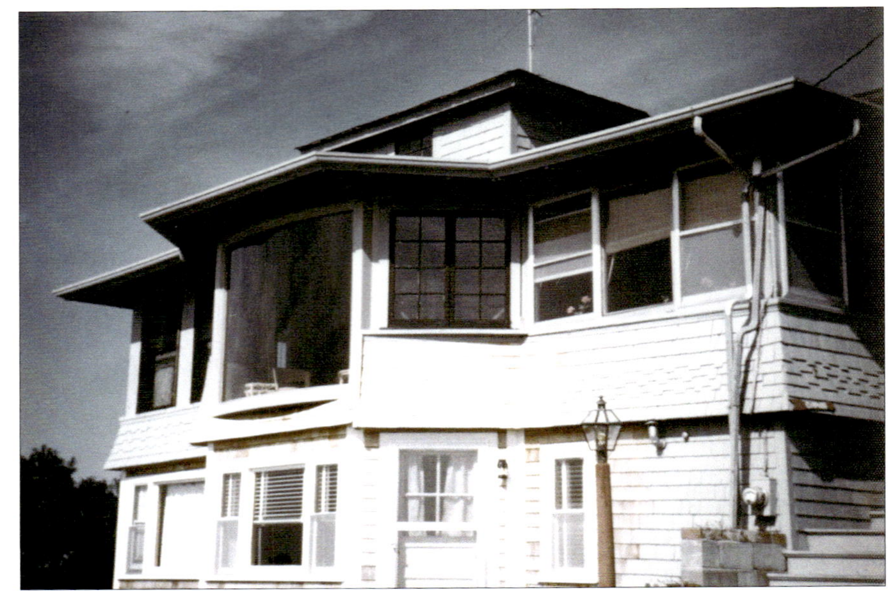

Land's End Inn, circa 1960

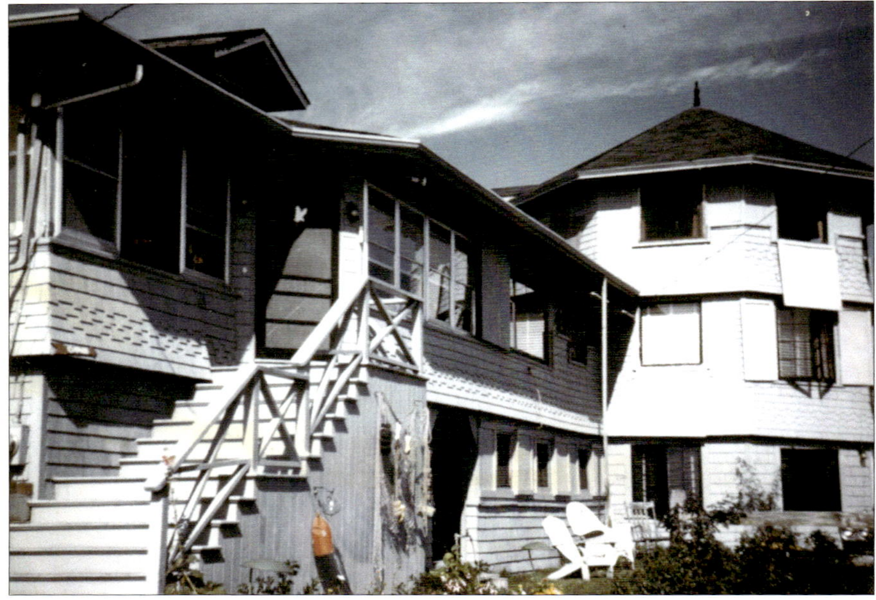

Land's End Inn, circa 1960

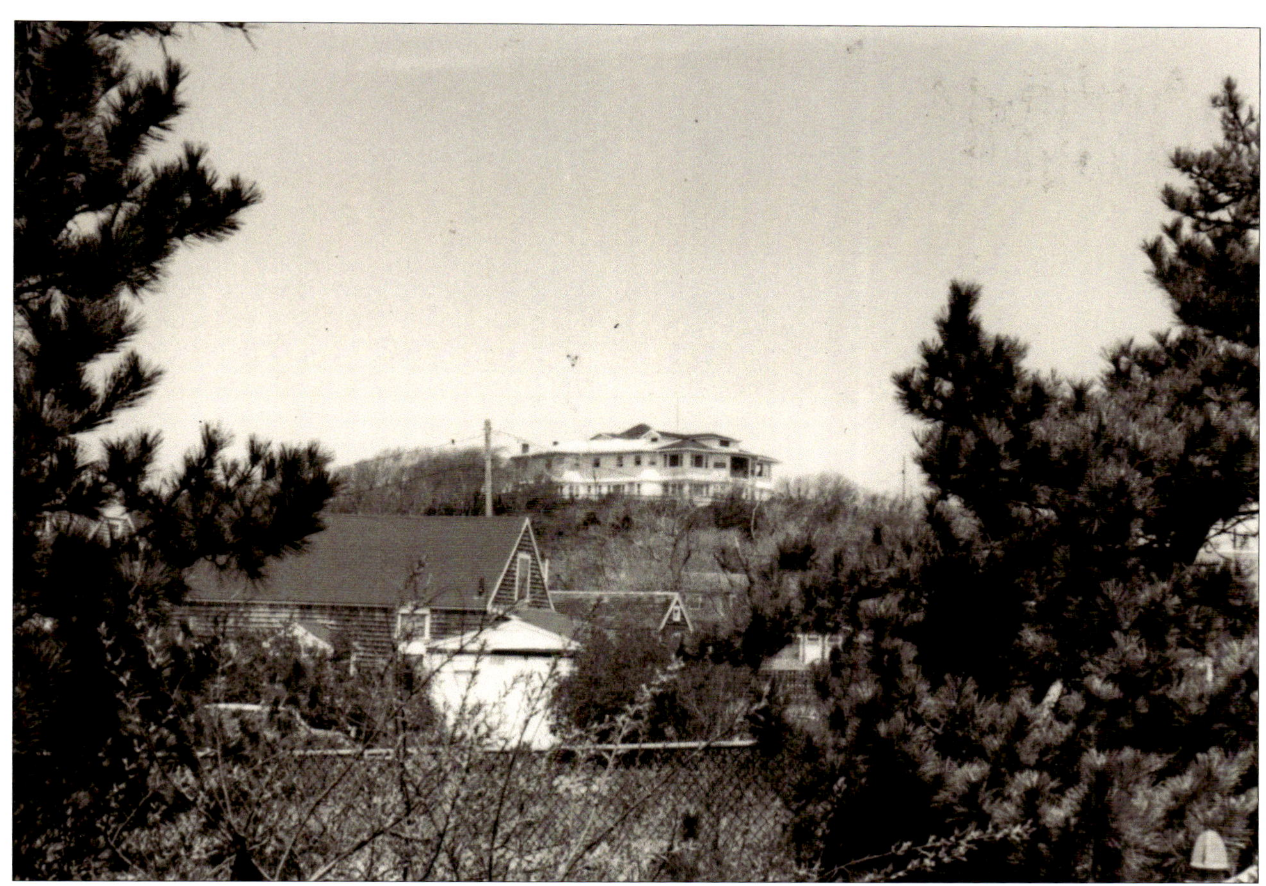

Land's End Inn, circa 1965

David's House... Bohemia

In 1972, David Schoolman purchased Land's End Inn sight unseen at the age of twenty-eight. He had graduated from Johns Hopkins University and Penn State with a master's degree in psychology and was working with troubled teens at the time. After vacationing in Provincetown, he fell in love with the community and determined to find an income-generating property to buy so he could move and live there full-time.

David brought unbelievable vision and a magical energy to the inn. He embellished its exterior while also preserving artisanal details and character throughout Higgins's creation. One of the first changes he made was to remove the vinyl siding added by the previous owners and restore Cape Cod shingles on the exterior. The other significant changes he made included adding the large veranda and new tower at the front of the building, extending the rooms on the main level, and adding private baths.

In the early 1980s, a friend of David's who was a landscape architect helping him with a plan for the gardens suggested that adding a veranda could enhance the inn by offering guests a place to lounge throughout the day. David wasted no time and started building the next day. There were no plans, just a vision in their heads.

David lived at the inn and made it a social hub for the Provincetown community. His annual parties would bring as many as six hundred people to the lawn. These much-anticipated, newsworthy celebrations spanned decades.

David's expansion of the house, collections, and parties helped define the inn. When he died of AIDS in 1995, the inn passed to the David Schoolman Trust, which he had organized to benefit the theater community in Provincetown. The trust ultimately sold the inn, and proceeds from the sale funded a $750,000 gift that helped to establish a permanent facility for the Provincetown Theater in the East End.

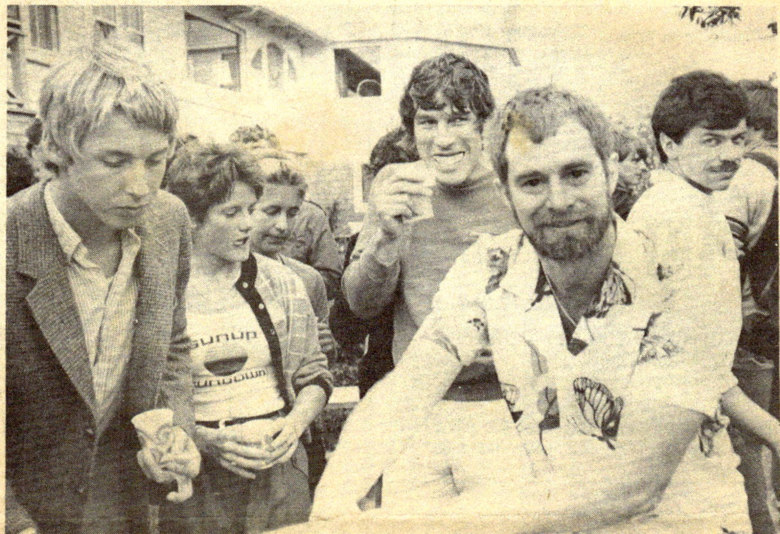

Photo by Jve

Land's End Party:

Summer is almost in full swing. All this talk of the Blessing of the Fleet and the Fourth of July — sure signs of summer. Another sure sign of summer is the Land's End Party.

This is a party that David Schoolman has been having at this Land's End guest house for the past 11 years. This year was no exception. About the only thing that *was* an exception was the weather, First of all, because it wasn't raining, something it had been doing quite a lot of lately. And second, because the day of the Land's End party is usually a bright and sunny day, a day that shows off the panoramic view of Provincetown and the bay. This day was cloudy and windy. However, the rain did hold off til after the party. The only time it ever rained on the party itself, David recalls, was back in 1975.

Land's End sits atop the highest part of Commercial Street in the far West End of town. The late Victorian house and the grounds are well manicured. Being up so high, and just about as far west as you can get, the view of the town and the bay is spectacular and makes a great place to celebrate the coming of the season. The house has 24 rooms to stroll through — a living room, solarium, guest rooms, even a rotunda room with windows on all sides. The view from there takes in sunrise over the bay, sunset over the dunes, the Cape's Lip, the ocean, the town… and if there is anything else you came to Provincetown to see, you can probably see it from there.

David's party happens every year just before the summer solstice. If you missed it this time, don't worry. The summer of 1983 can't be that far away.

PROVINCETOWN MAGAZINE 31

Clipping from Provincetown Magazine *covering David's annual summer party, 1982. David is on the right.*

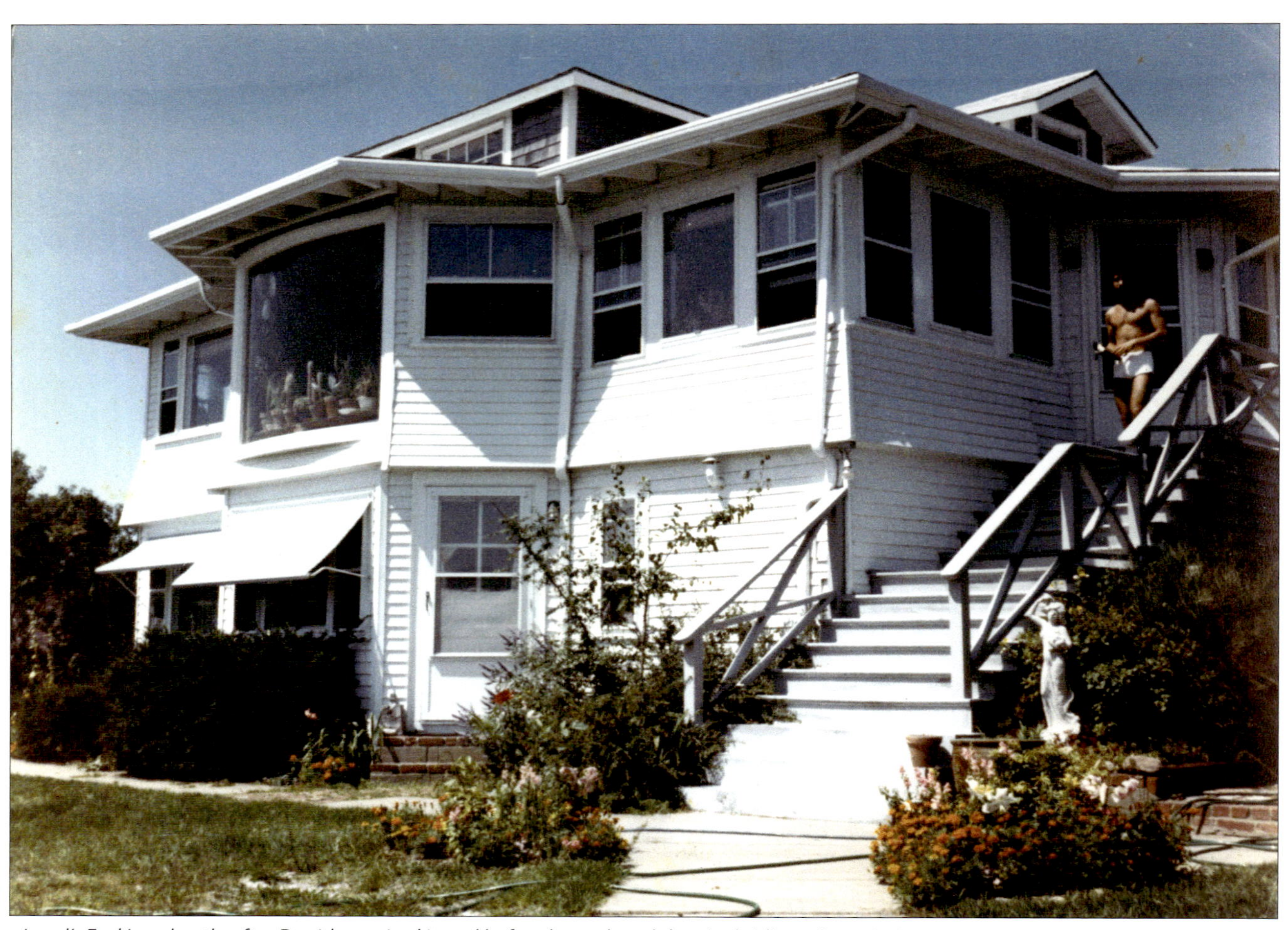

Land's End Inn shortly after David acquired it and before he replaced the vinyl siding, circa 1972

We heard the property was available on a Saturday, and we signed the papers the following Monday. I took a two-hour course in laundry and a few other things from the owners of George's Inn and went into business.

- David Schoolman

Elaborately designed, elegant brochures, party invitations, and holiday cards were a signature element of David's Land's End Inn.

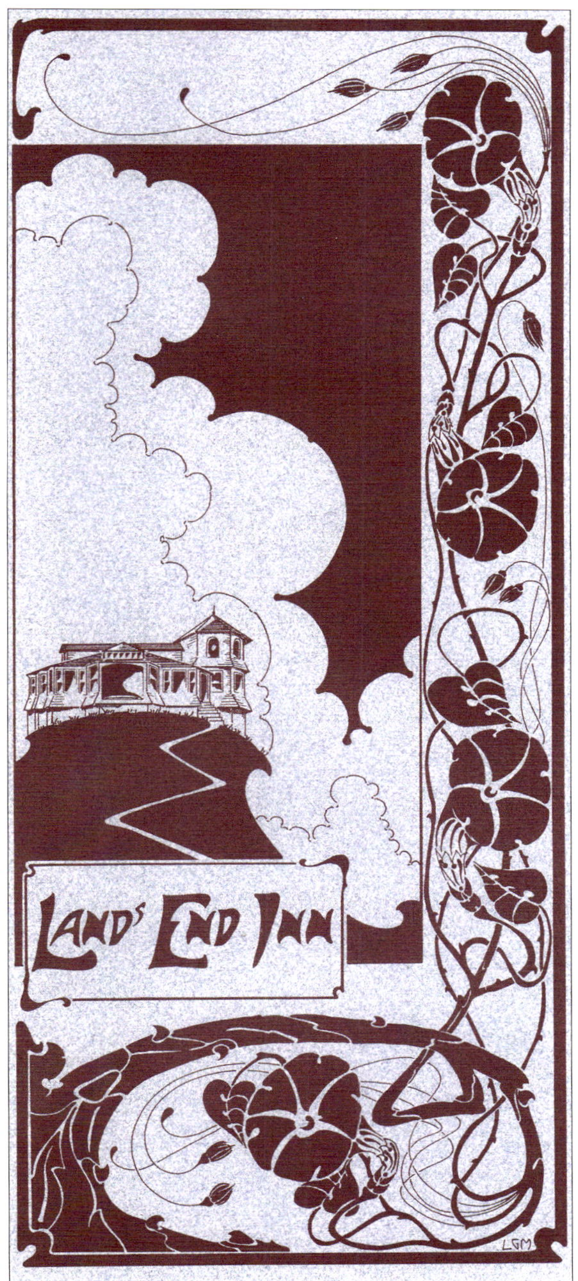

Brochure, circa 1980

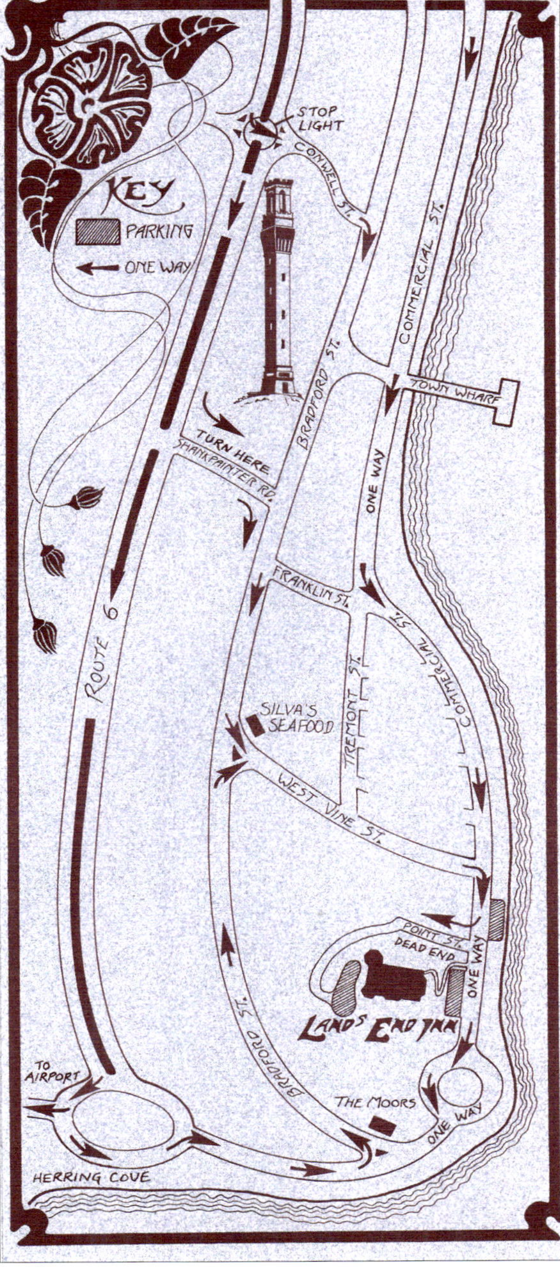

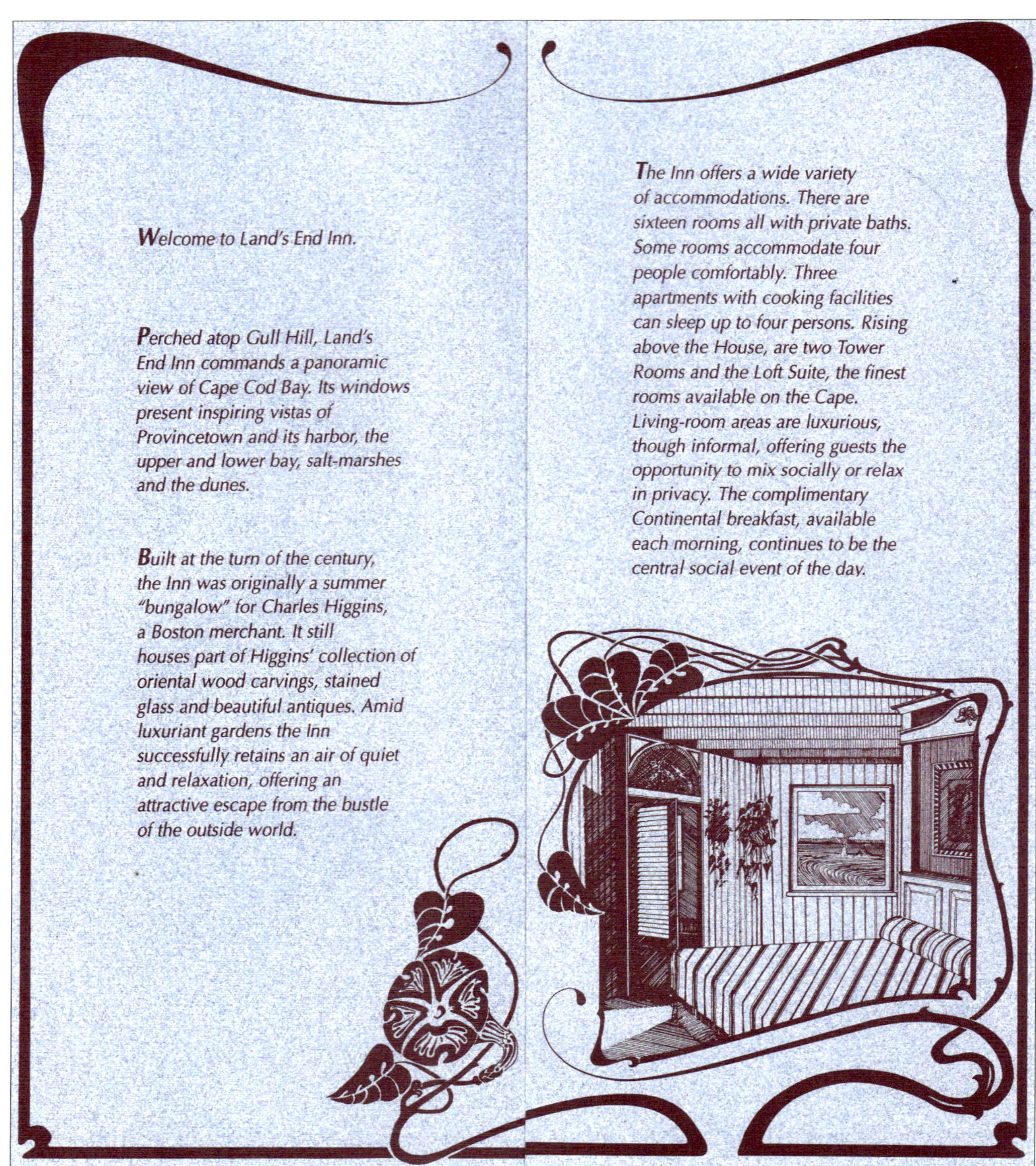

Brochure, circa 1980

42

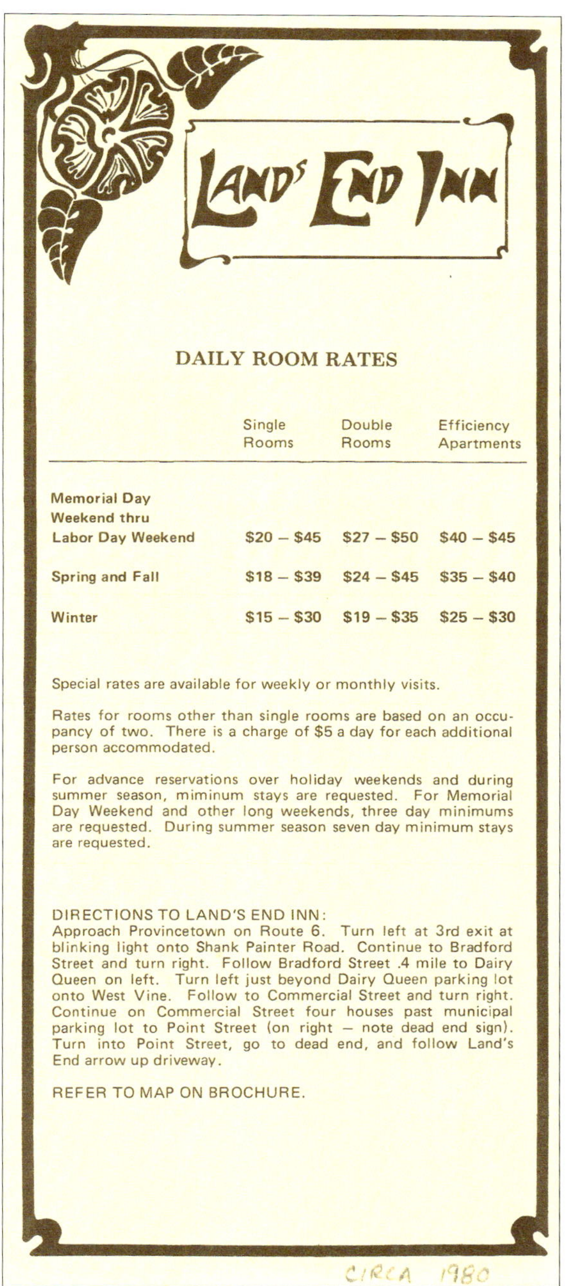

	Single Rooms	Double Rooms	Efficiency Apartments
Memorial Day Weekend thru Labor Day Weekend	$20 — $45	$27 — $50	$40 — $45
Spring and Fall	$18 — $39	$24 — $45	$35 — $40
Winter	$15 — $30	$19 — $35	$25 — $30

Rate card, circa 1980

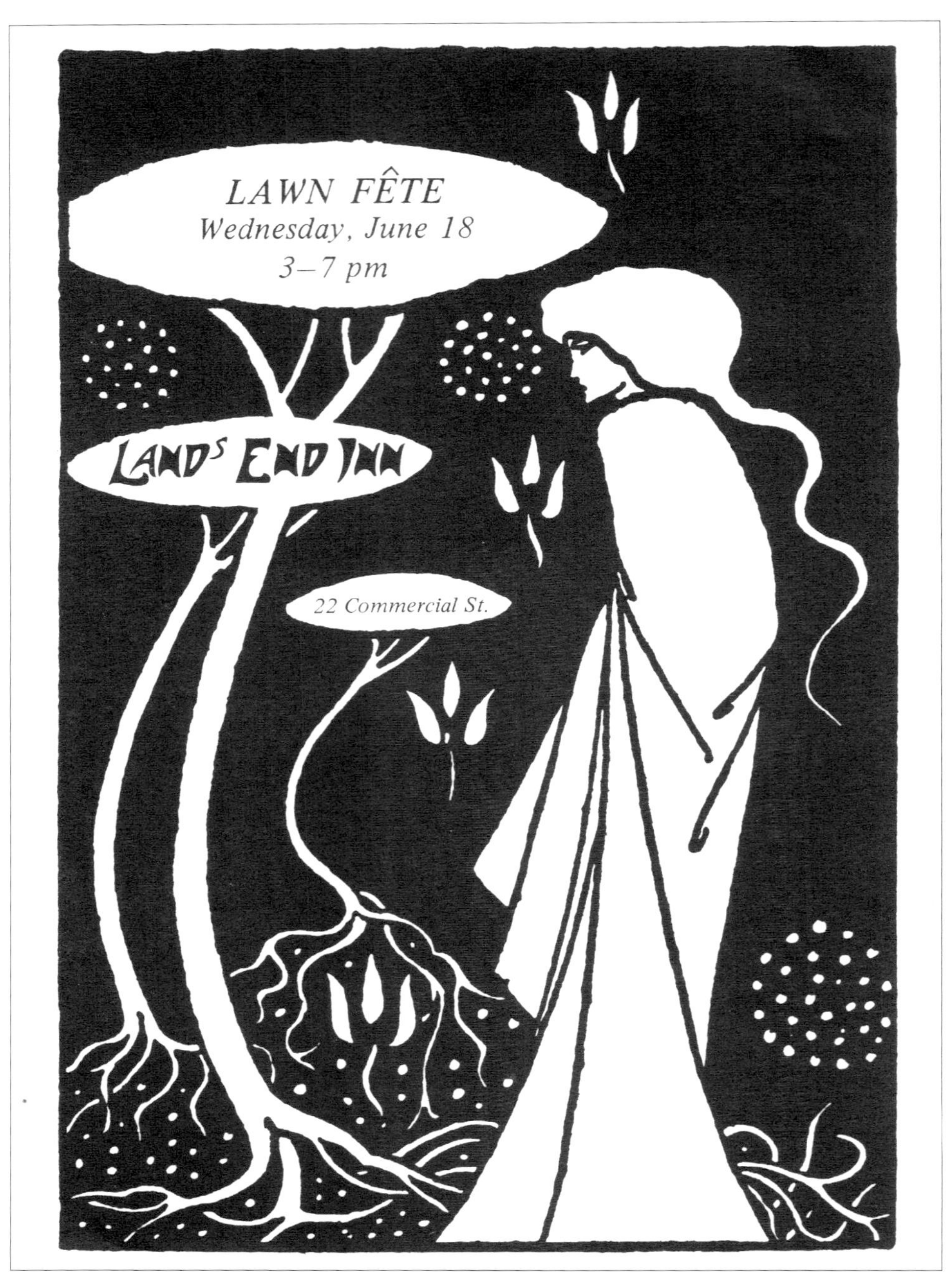

Invitation to one of David's annual parties, circa 1979

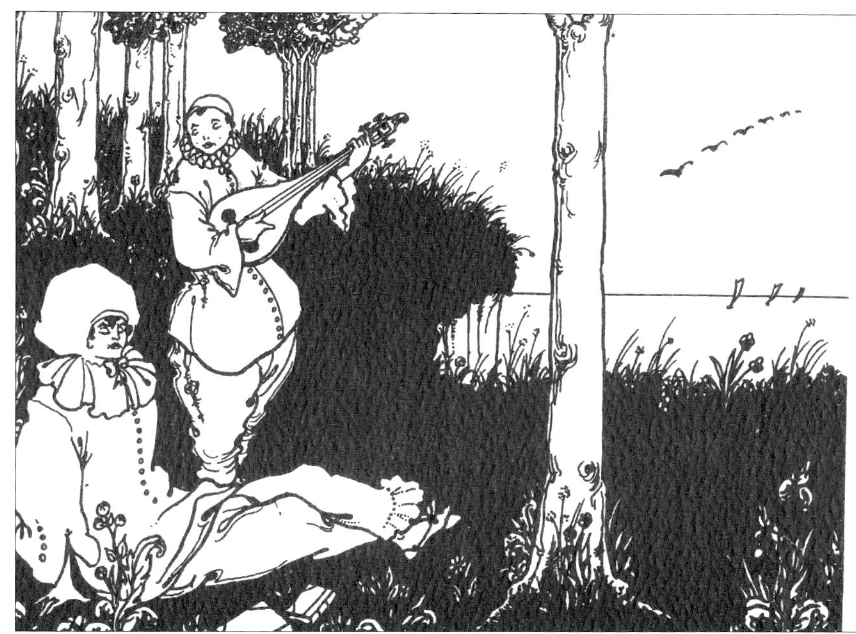

Invitation to one of David's annual parties, circa 1979

David Schoolman sure knows how to throw a party. He had no trouble getting at least 600 persons to his Land's End Inn for his fifth annual open lawn party. It has become a party for dressing up.

- *Provincetown Advocate*, 1976

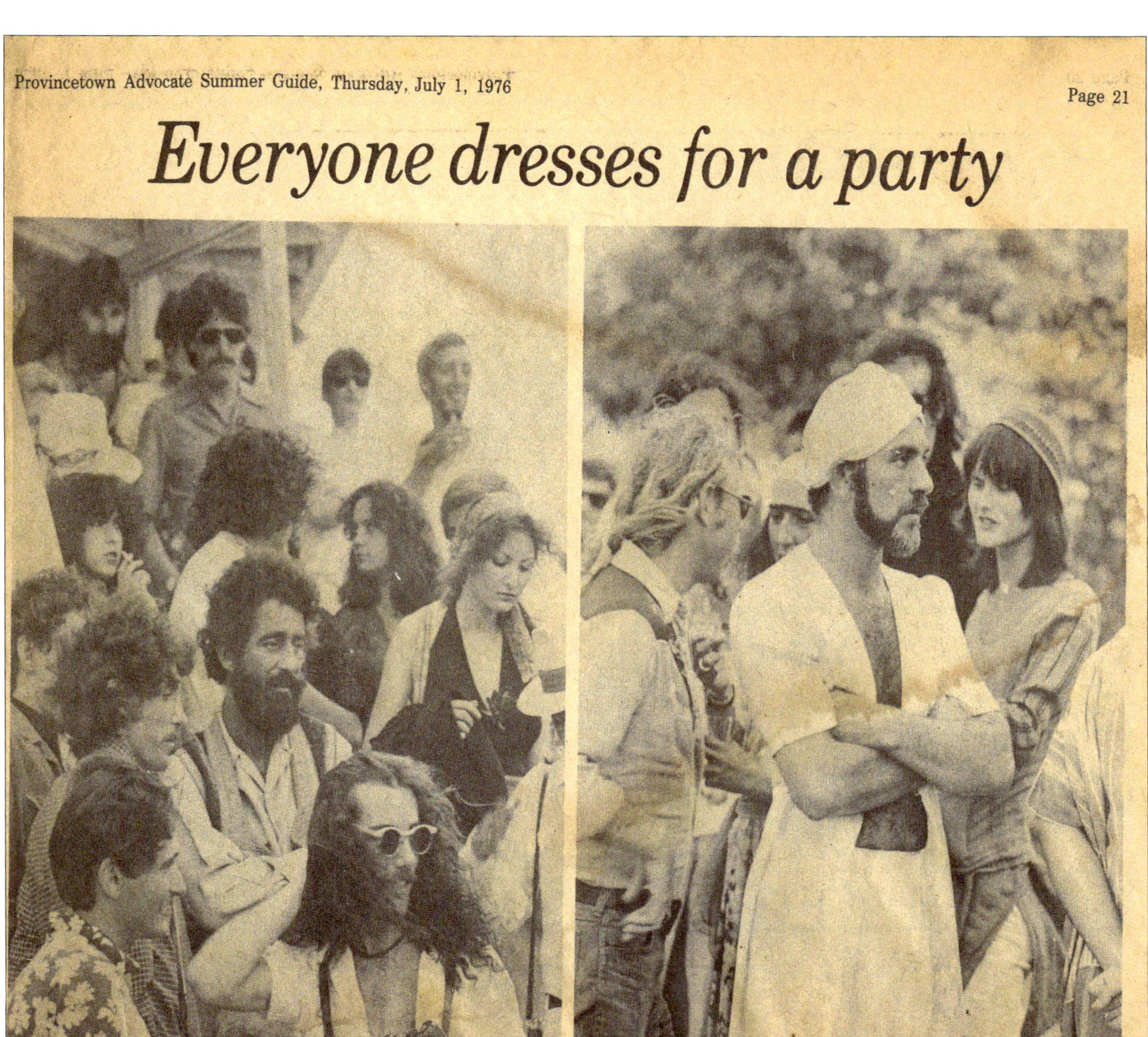

Clipping from the Provincetown Advocate Summer Guide *covering David's annual summer party, 1976*

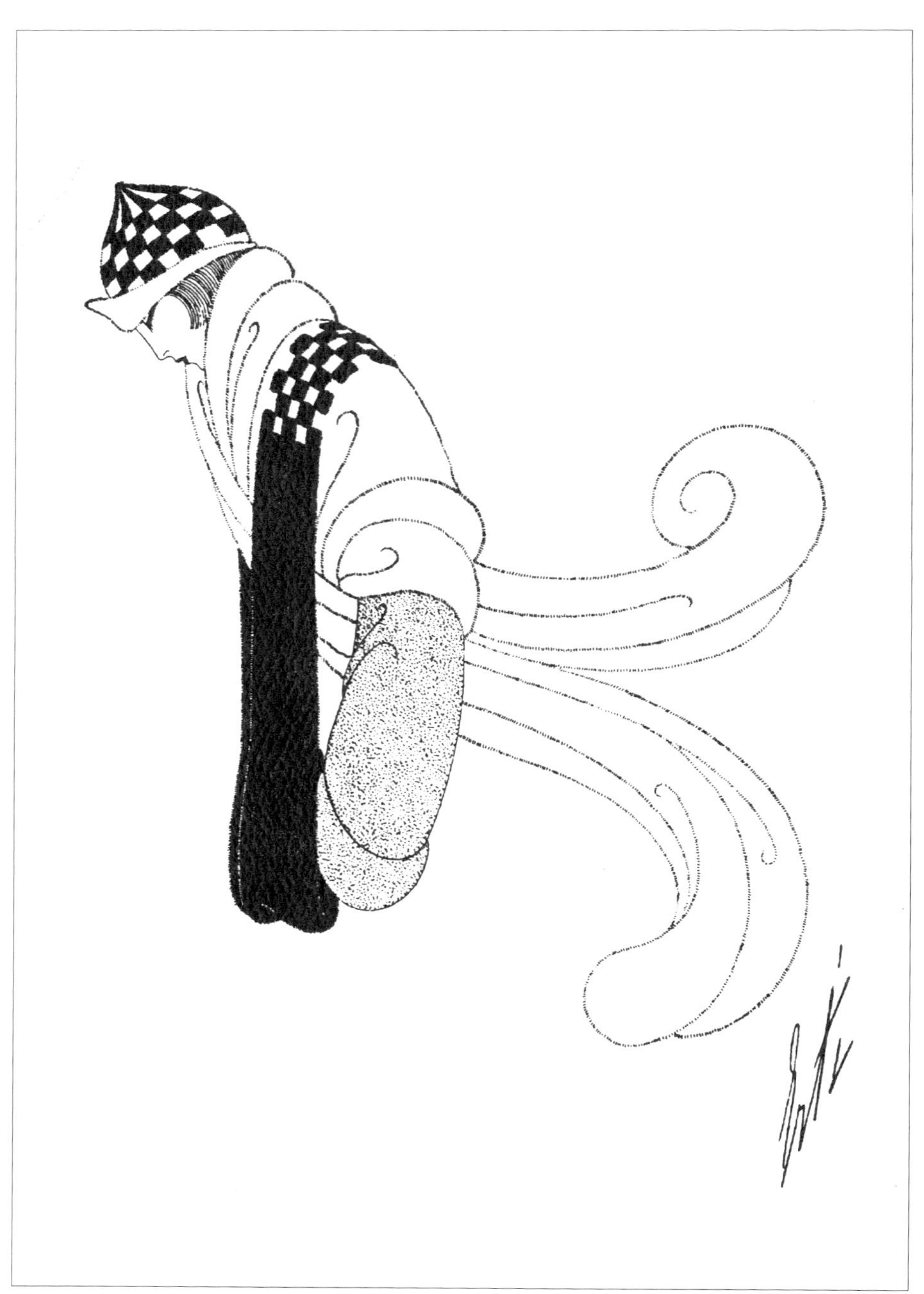

Holiday card, circa 1980. Original design by Erté, 1923.

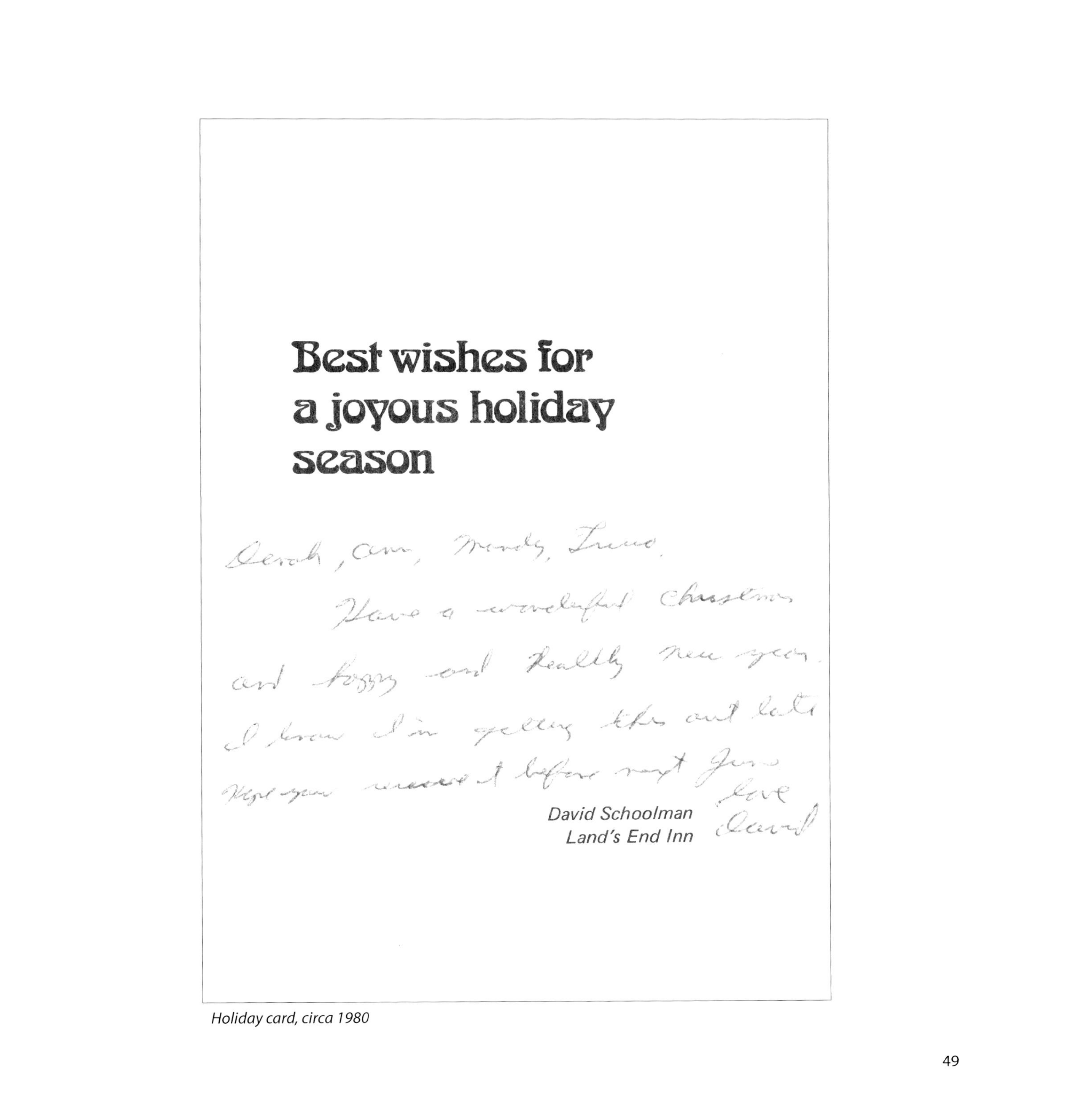

Best wishes for a joyous holiday season

David Schoolman
Land's End Inn

Holiday card, circa 1980

I put all my energies into this place. It's a full winter's project keeping it in shape, rebuilding, changing things. During the summer, there just isn't time, just too many people... They come from all over—Canada, New York, the Midwest. I love meeting new people and learning about them.

- David Schoolman

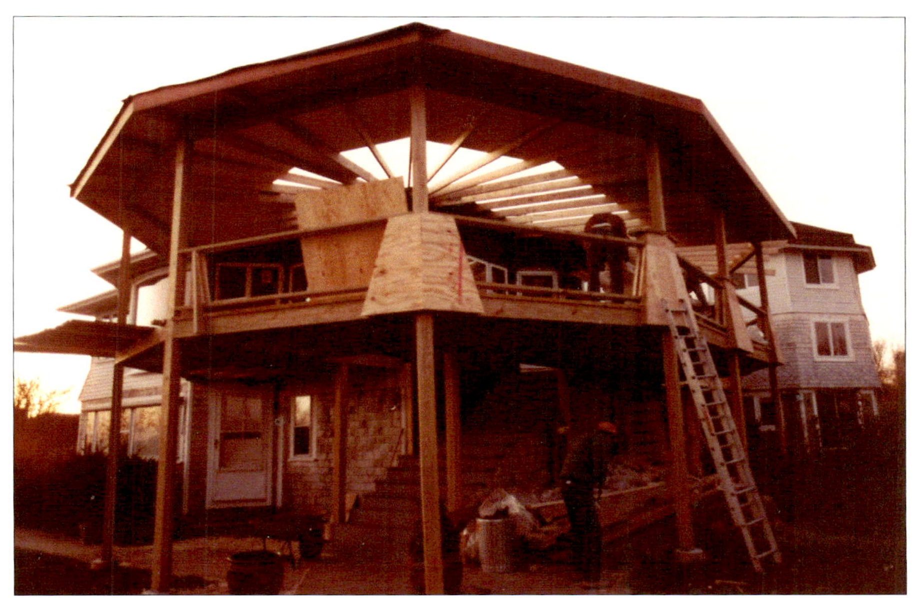

Addition of the veranda, circa 1982

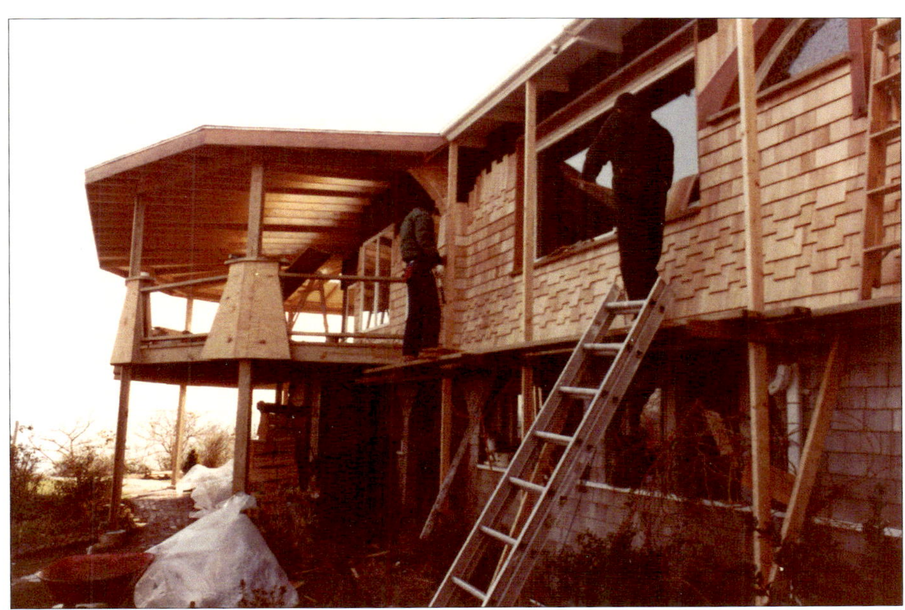

Addition of the veranda, circa 1982

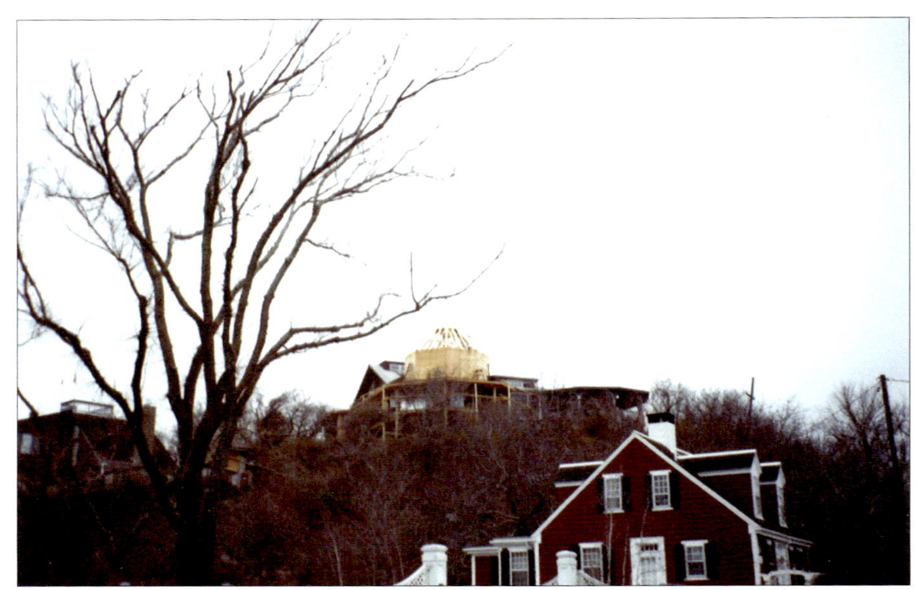

Addition of the Bay Tower Room, seen from the Red Inn, circa 1993

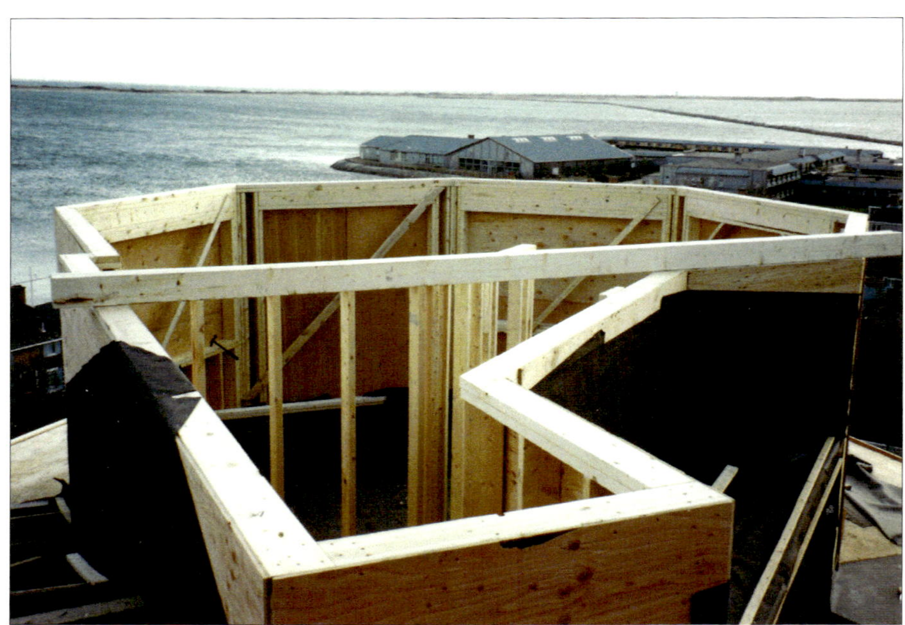

Framing for the addition of the Bay Tower Room, circa 1993. Note the Provincetown Inn in the background, with its then-covered pool house.

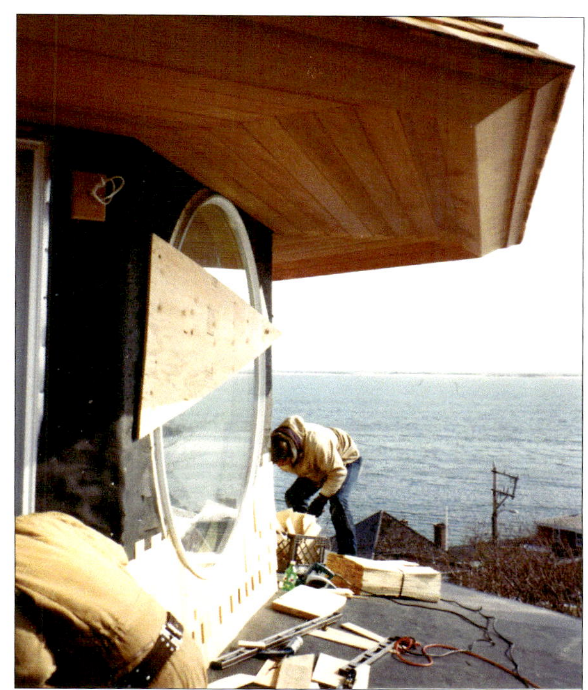

Addition of the Bay Tower Room, circa 1993

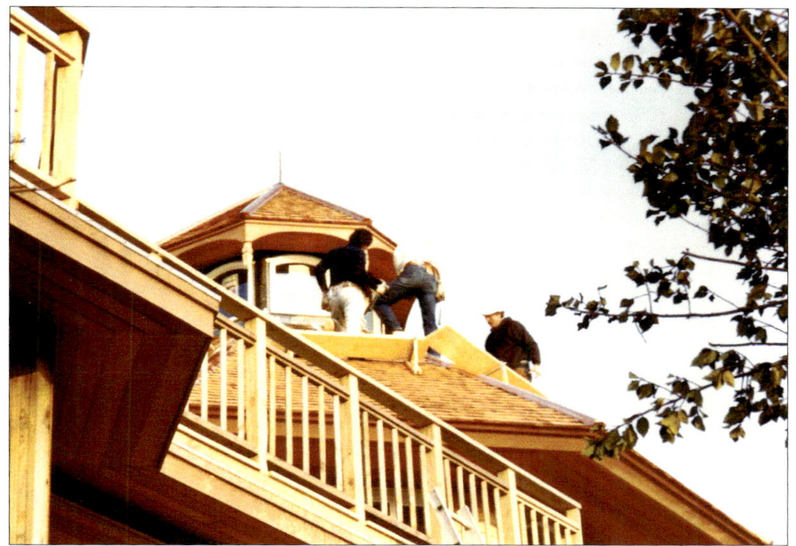

Addition of the Bay Tower Room, circa 1993

I like to think of Land's End as an excellent bouillabaisse—
everything goes together wonderfully.

- David Schoolman

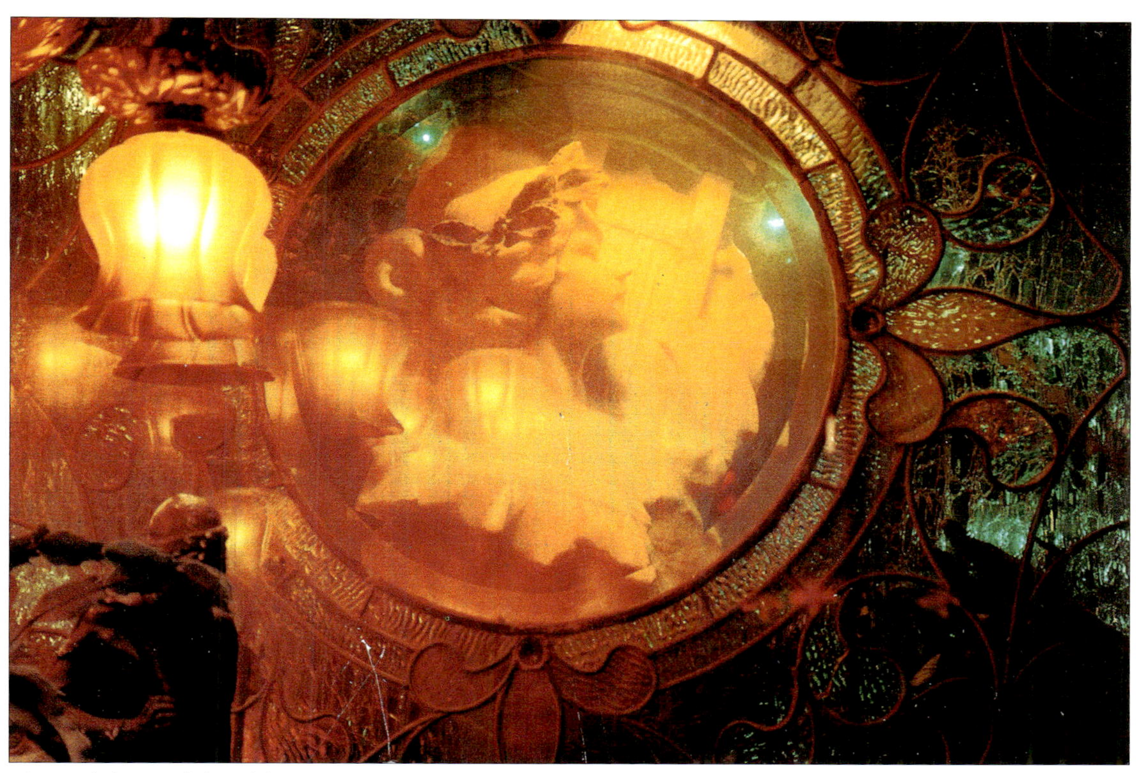

Stained glass and chandelier, circa 1990

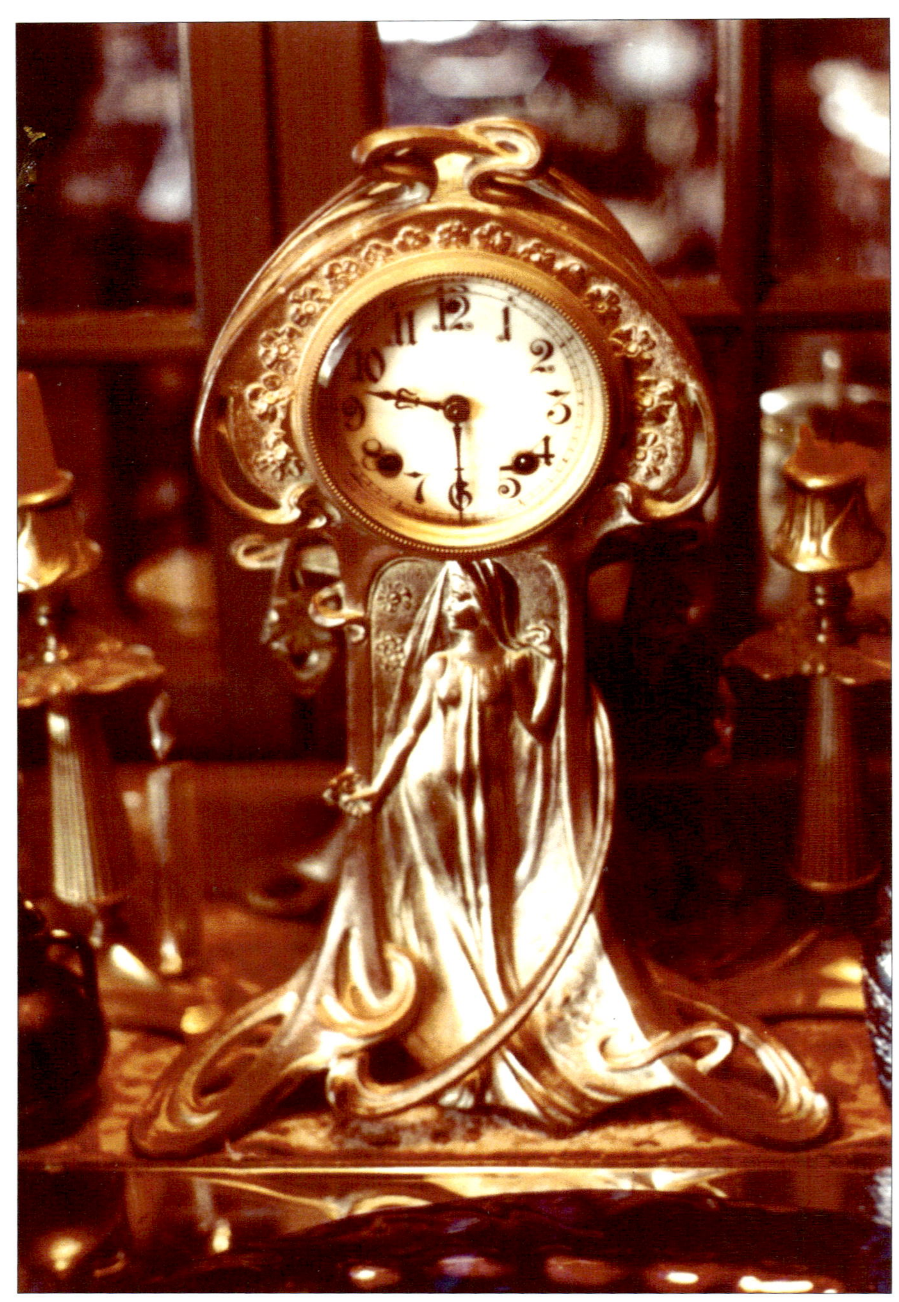

Clock, circa 1990

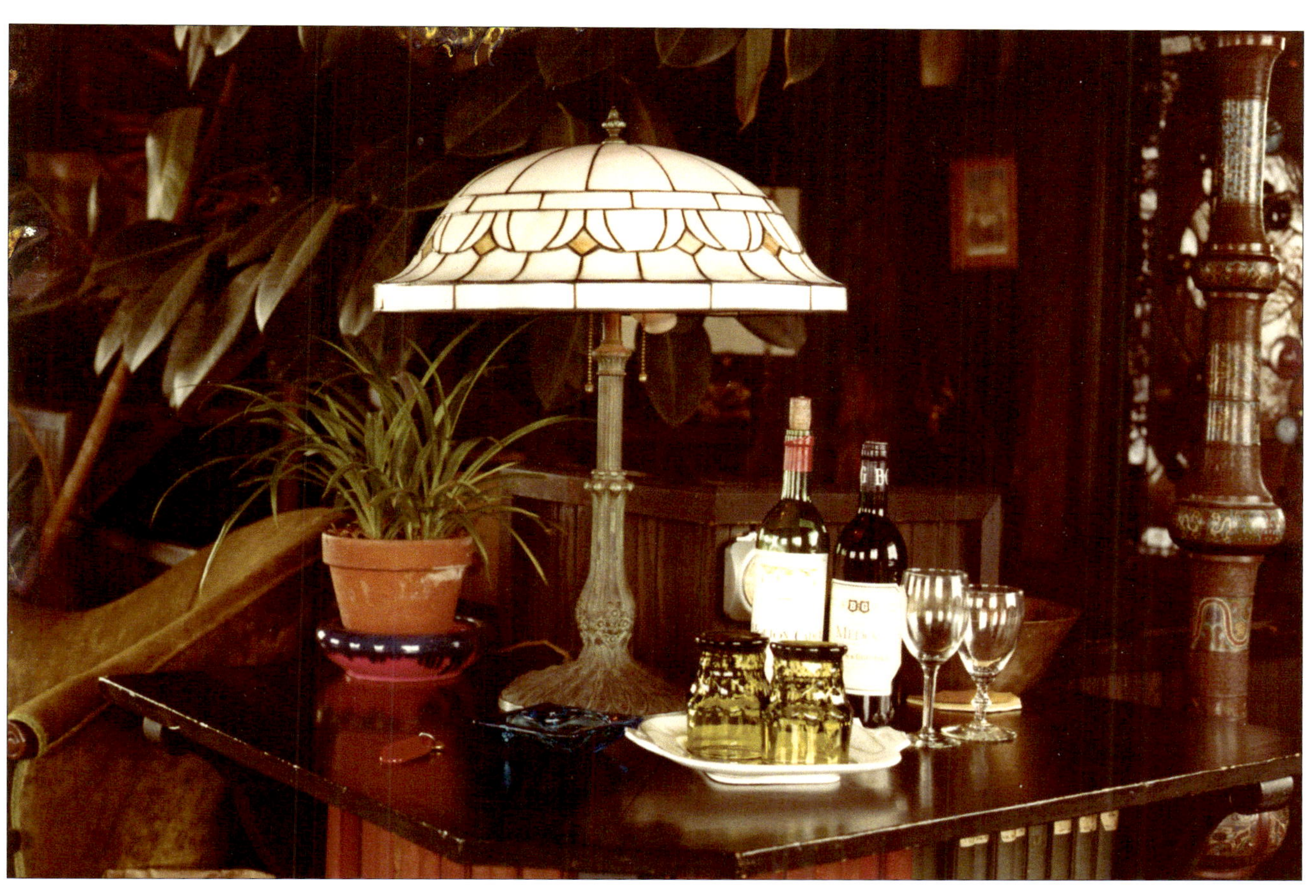

Wine service in the Moroccan Tower Room, circa 1990

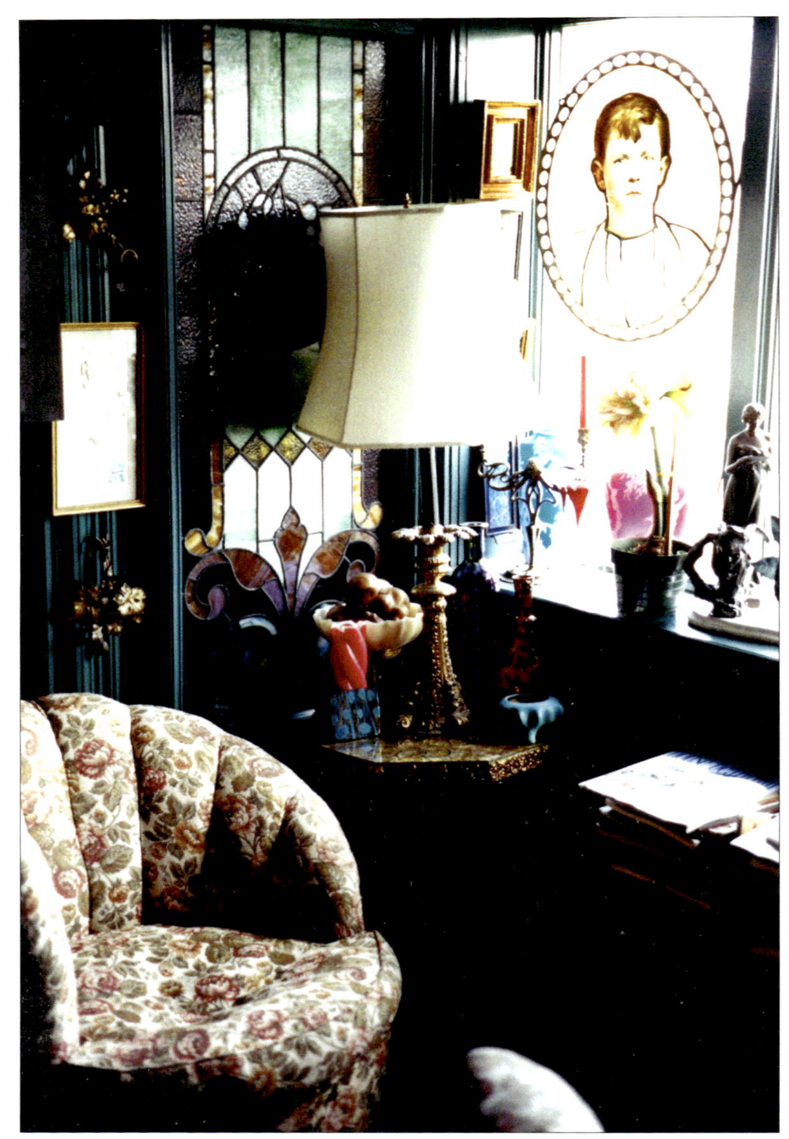

Sitting area, circa 1990

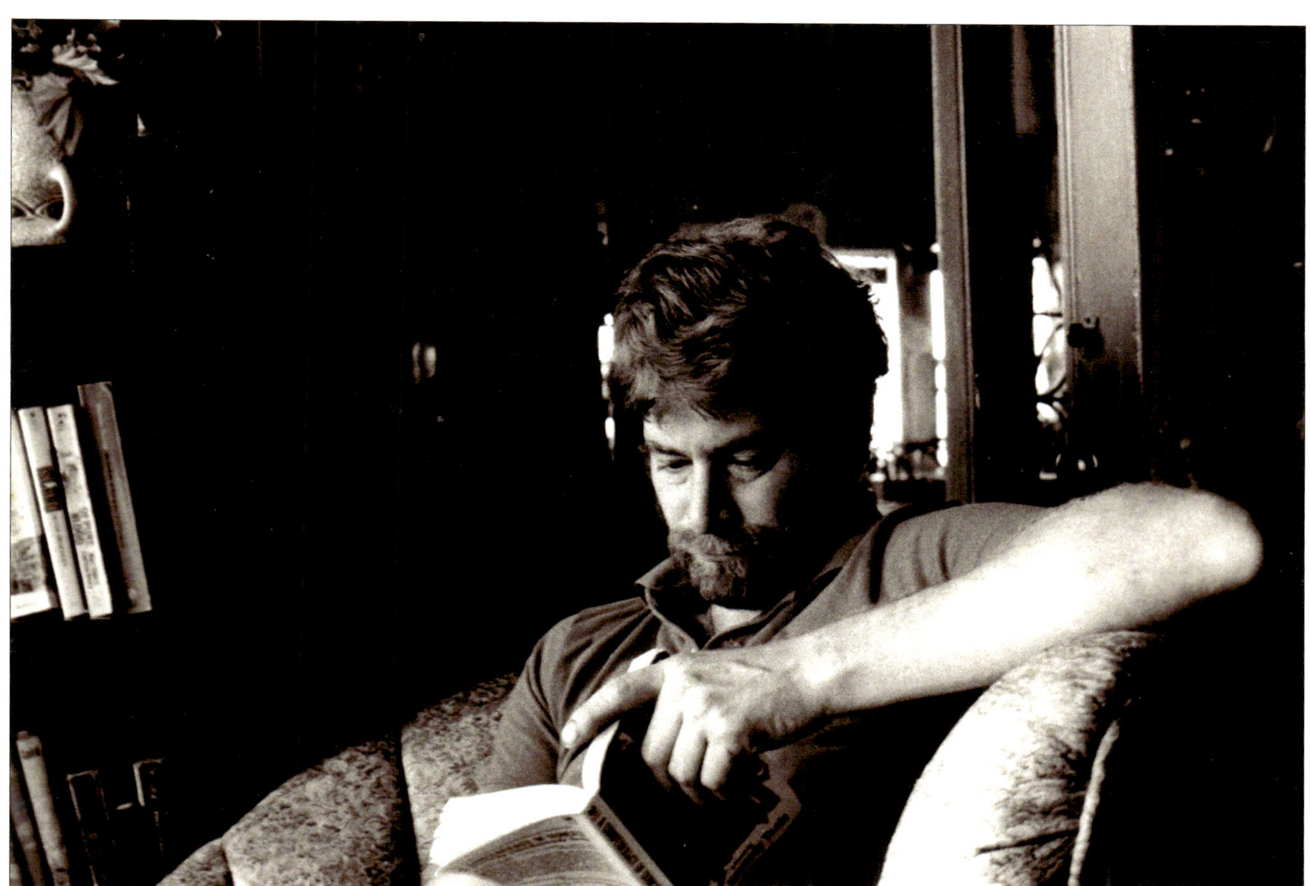

David Schoolman, circa 1990

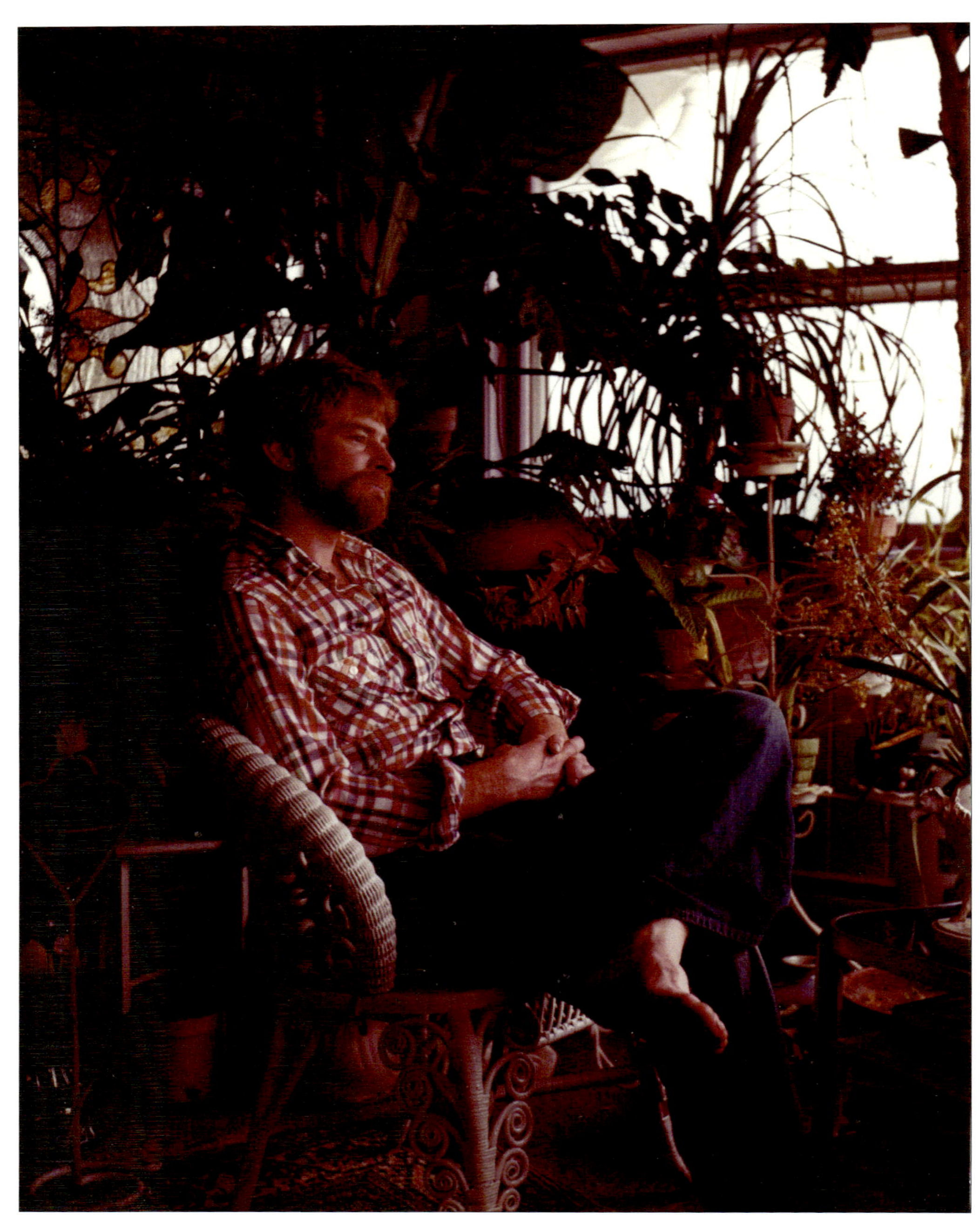

David Schoolman in the Solarium, circa 1994

David's House

Over the day
david plays
house of corners
hold little treats
urge refreshed spirits
through rooms
in crystal balls
hover at night
in the fog.

Ron Zullig

David Schoolman has left this town a lasting legacy. Before his death… Schoolman formed a not-for-profit trust to oversee the operation of the Land's End Inn… and to disperse the profits from that operation for the benefit of the performing arts in Provincetown.

- Provincetown Banner, 1995

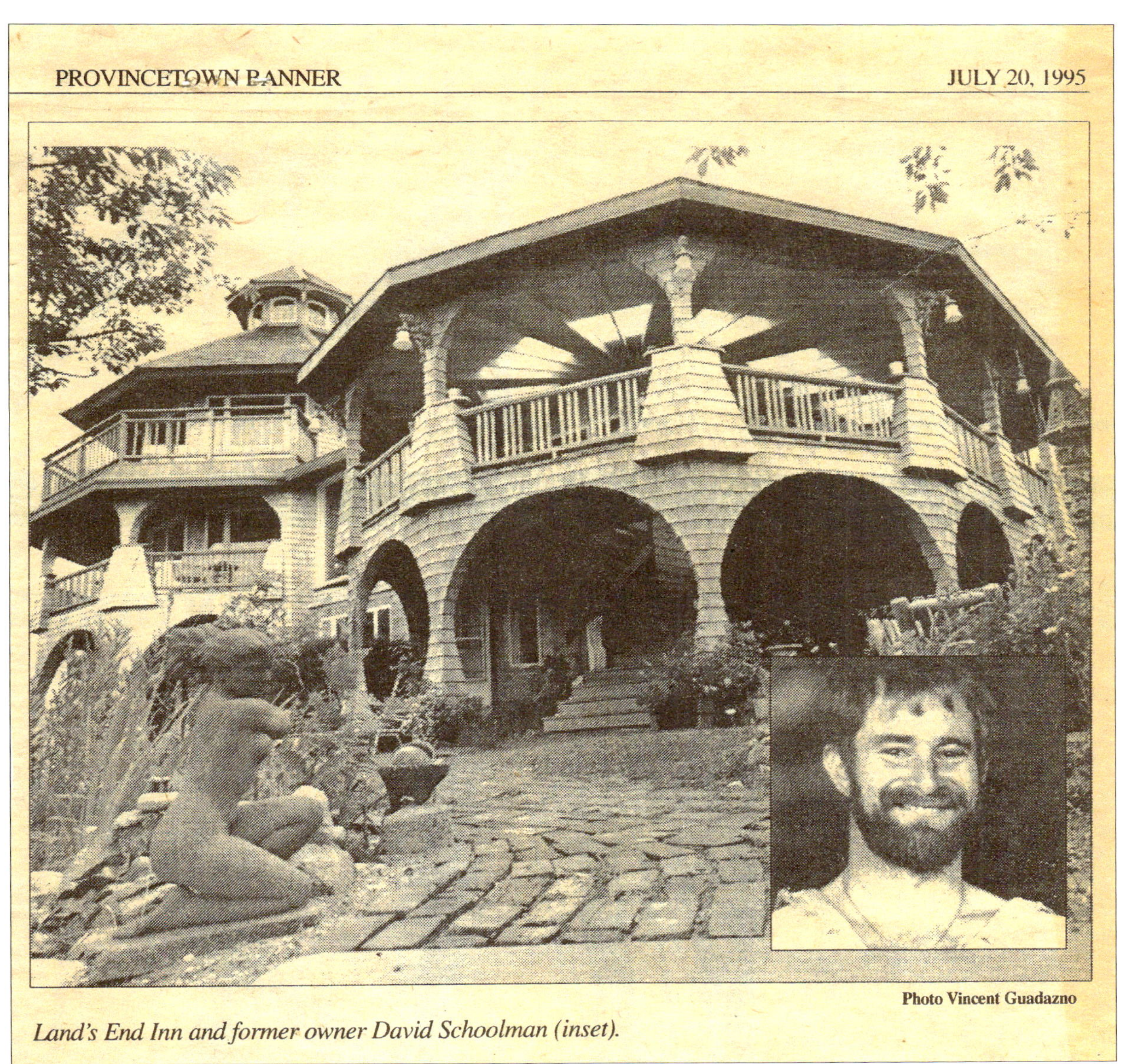

Photo Vincent Guadazno

Land's End Inn and former owner David Schoolman (inset).

Clipping from the Provincetown Banner *covering David's bequest to benefit local performing arts, 1995*

MacIntyre and Sikorski... Into the Next Century

Although David Schoolman intended for the charitable trust he had established to continue operating the inn after his passing, the trustees determined that selling the inn would enable the biggest impact. They sold the inn to Michael MacIntyre in 2001.

Michael committed himself to preserving the inn's integrity as a Provincetown landmark. An architecture buff, Michael integrated some of today's comforts and amenities, such as luxury bedding, upgraded indoor plumbing, and air conditioning, while consciously working to preserve the heritage and history associated with the inn. He enlarged the decks for expanded panoramic water views, reinvigorated the gardens, and added comfortable outdoor wicker furniture. Using plans developed by David Schoolman, he had local stonemasons relay the entrance path and walls.

Michael sold the inn to Stan and Eva Sikorski in 2012. The Sikorskis were world travelers and art lovers, and Provincetown had been a treasured part of their lives for more than forty-five years. They continued the high standards Land's End Inn guests had come to love and the previous owners' tradition of supporting the arts community through regular fundraisers and direct support for local charities and individual visual and performance artists.

MacIntyre and the Sikorskis invested heavily in the inn, bringing its infrastructure and amenities into the twenty-first century while also protecting its history and magical allure.

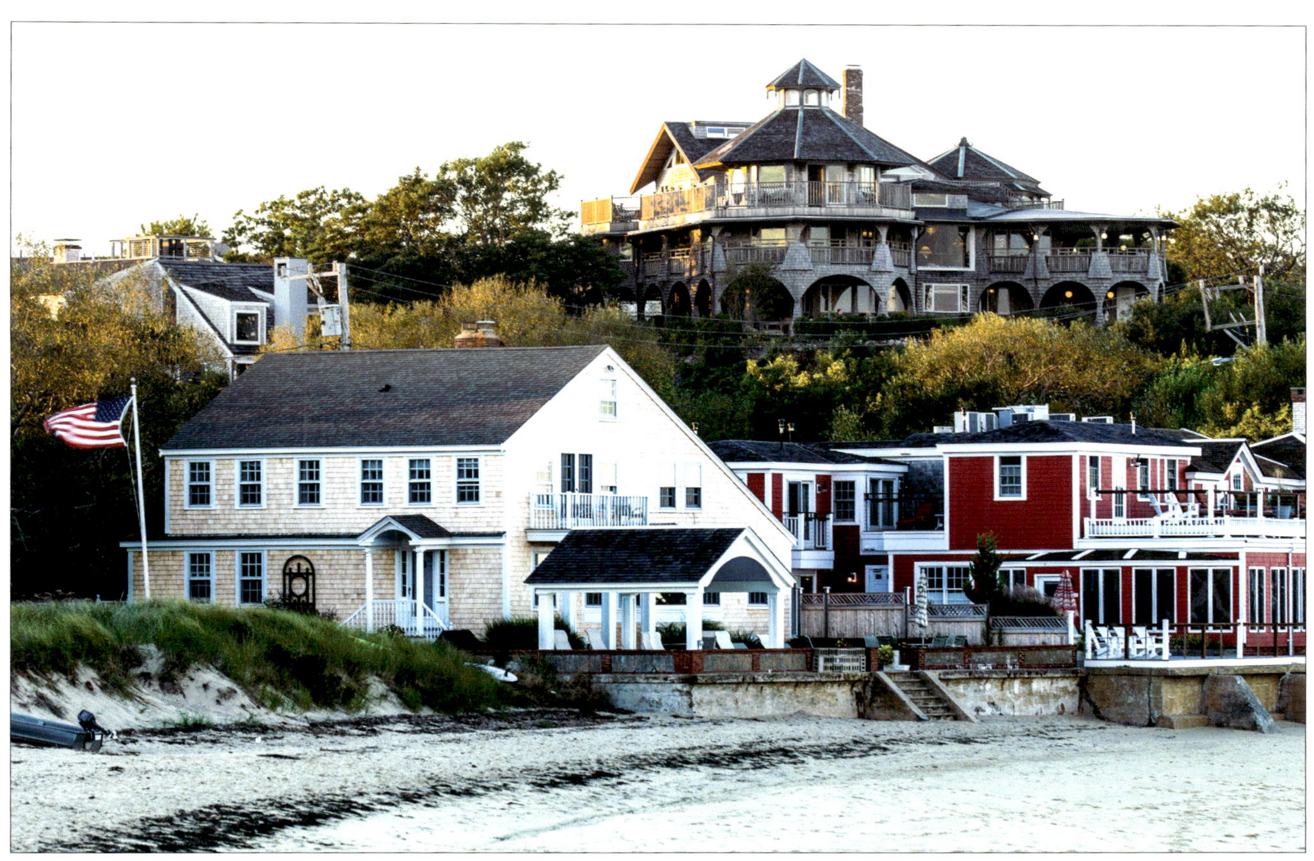

Land's End Inn perched on Gull Hill above the Red Inn, 2013

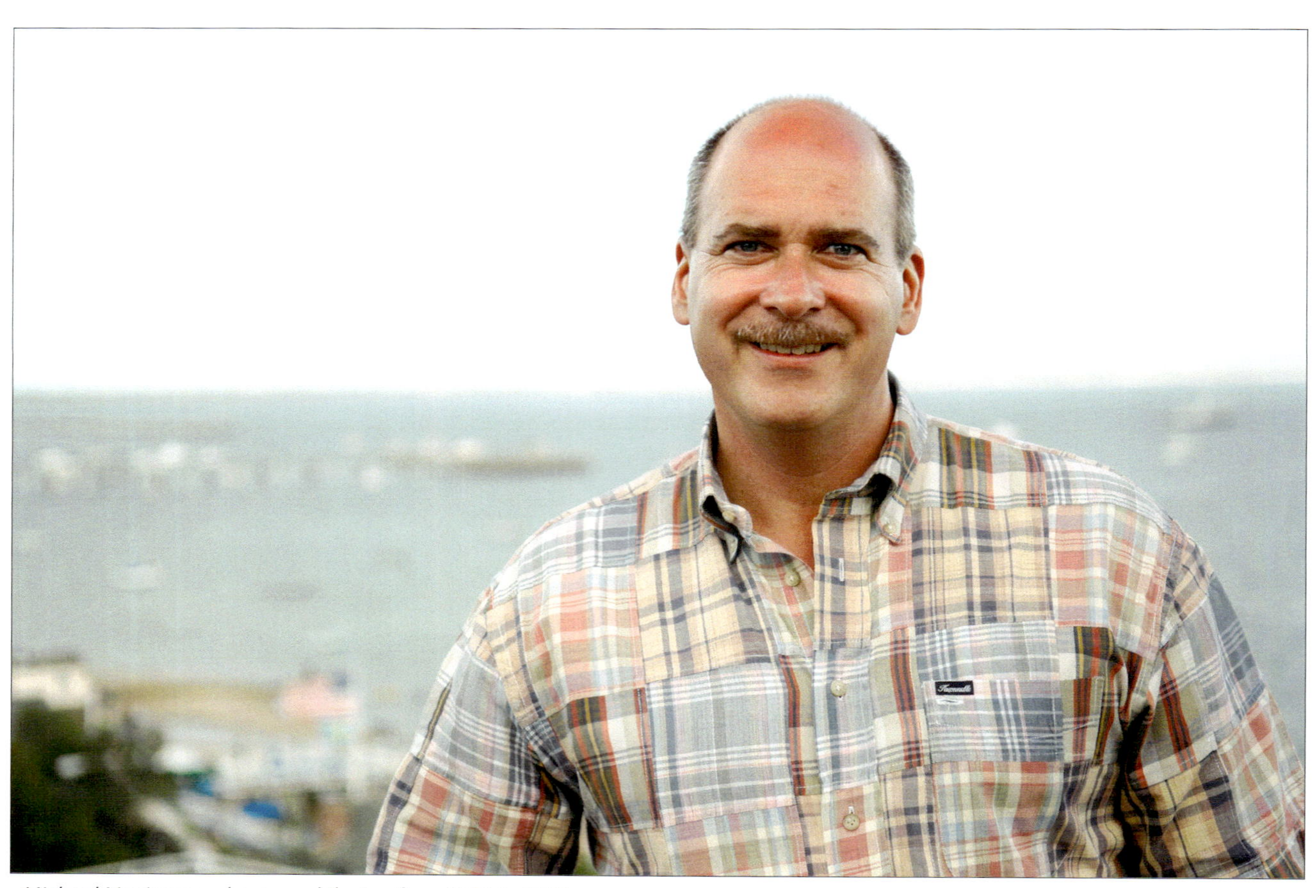

Michael MacIntyre, who owned the inn from 2001 to 2012

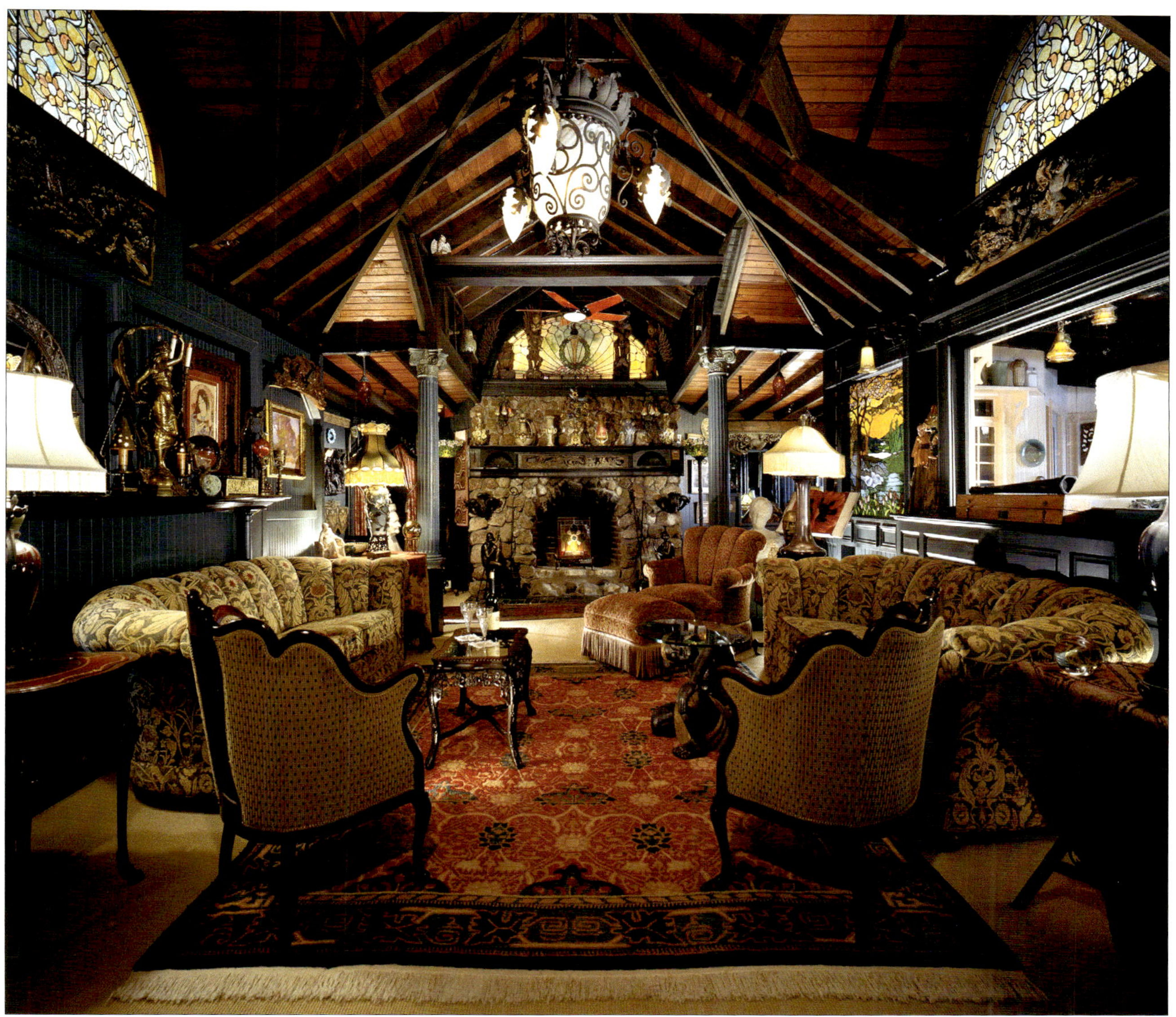

Great Room, 2004

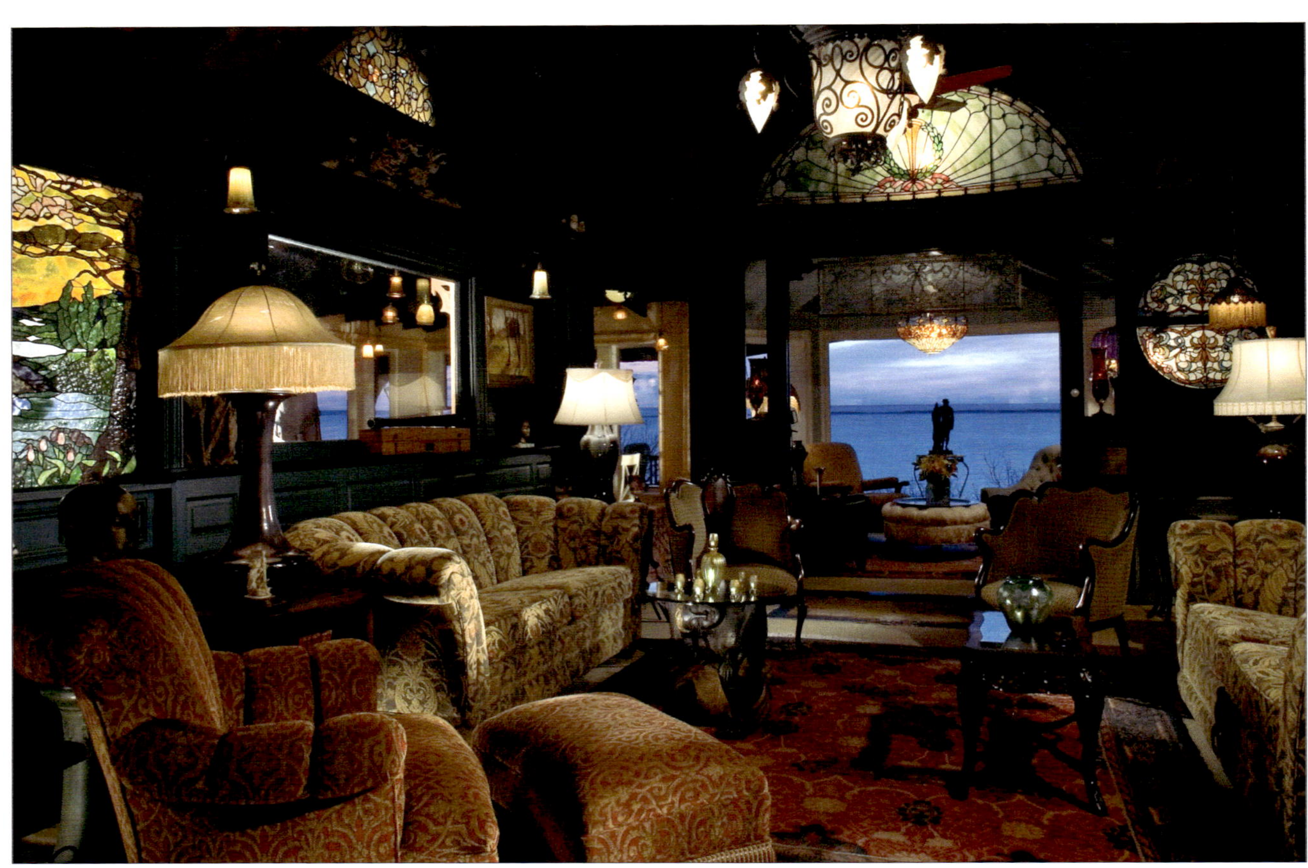

Great Room, 2004

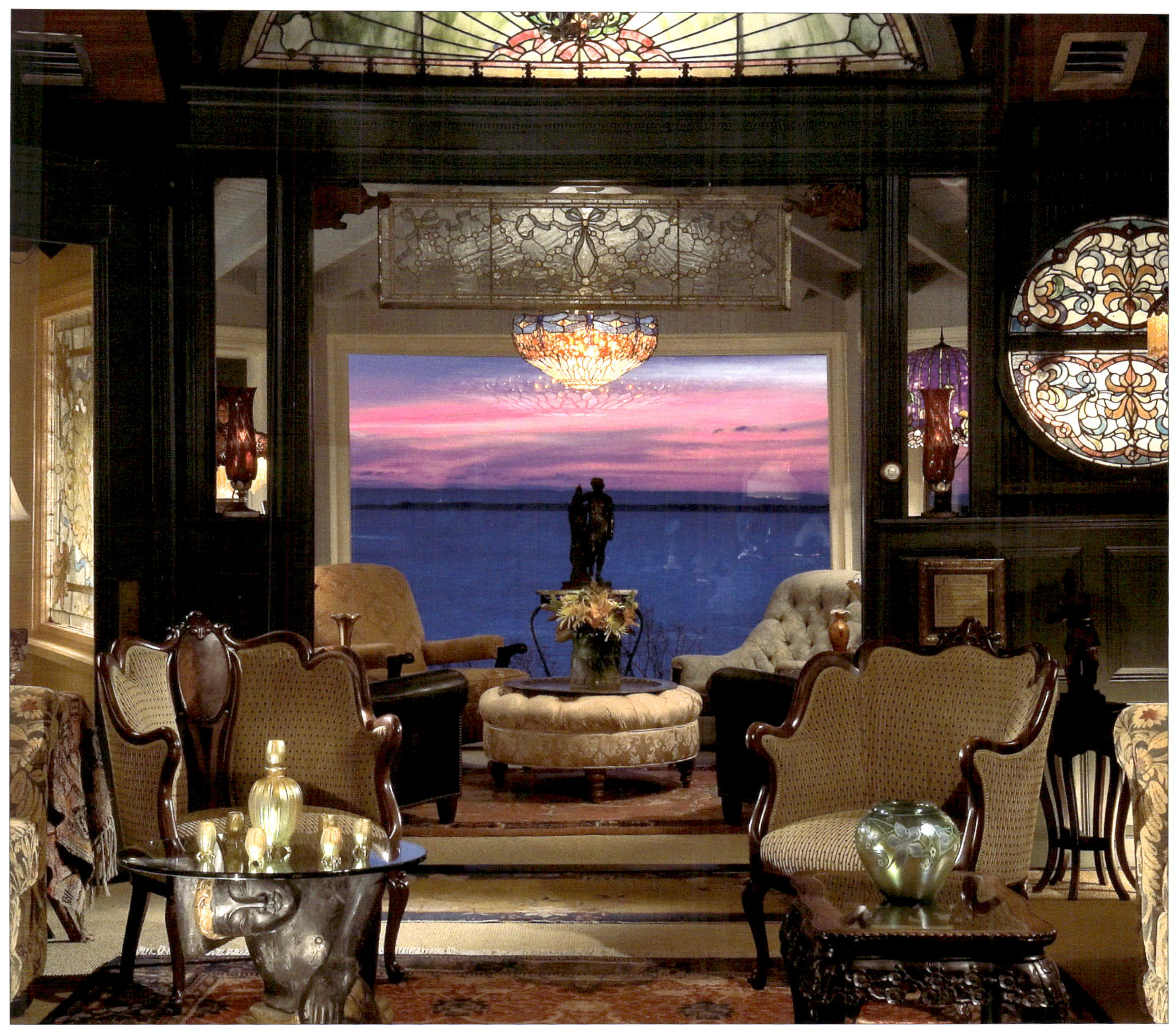

Solarium, 2004

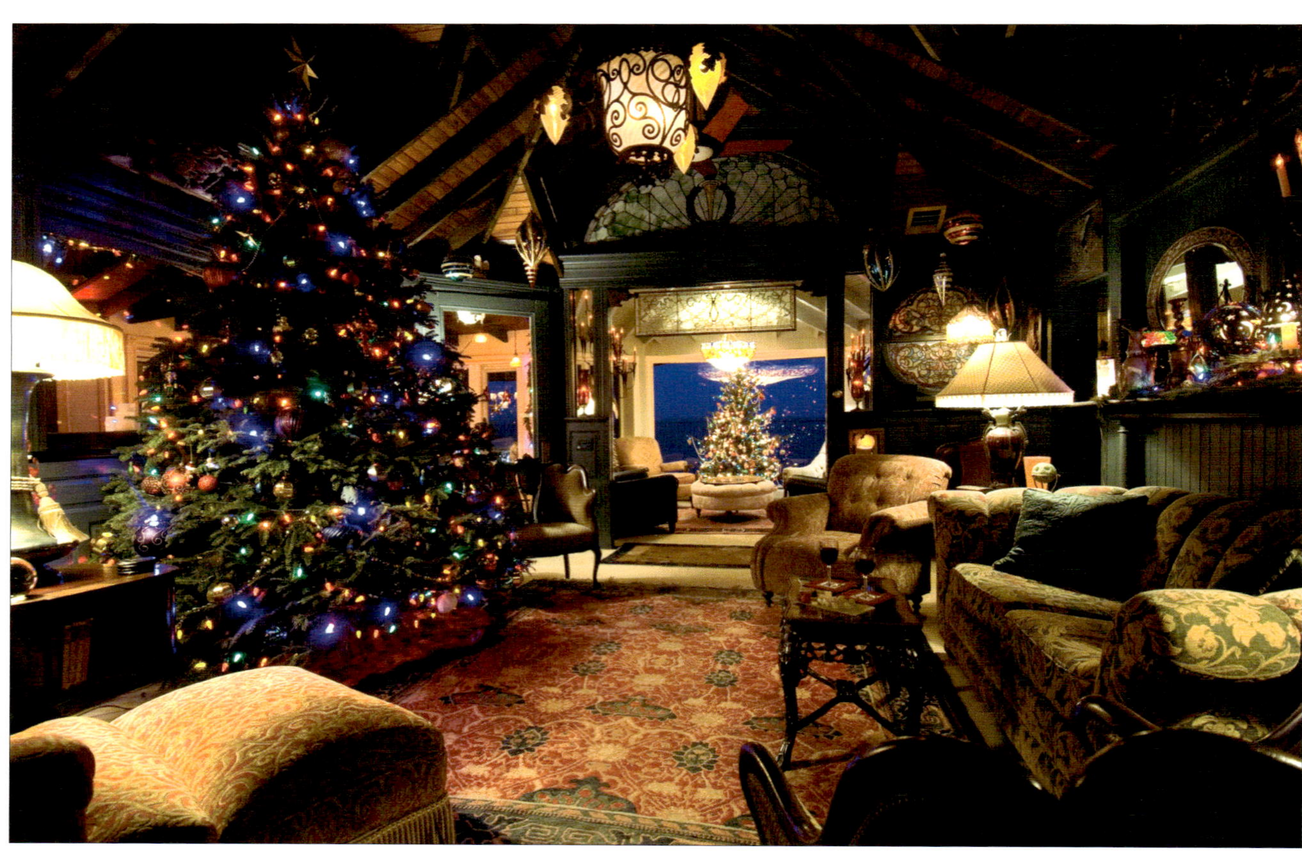

Great Room decorated for the holidays, 2008

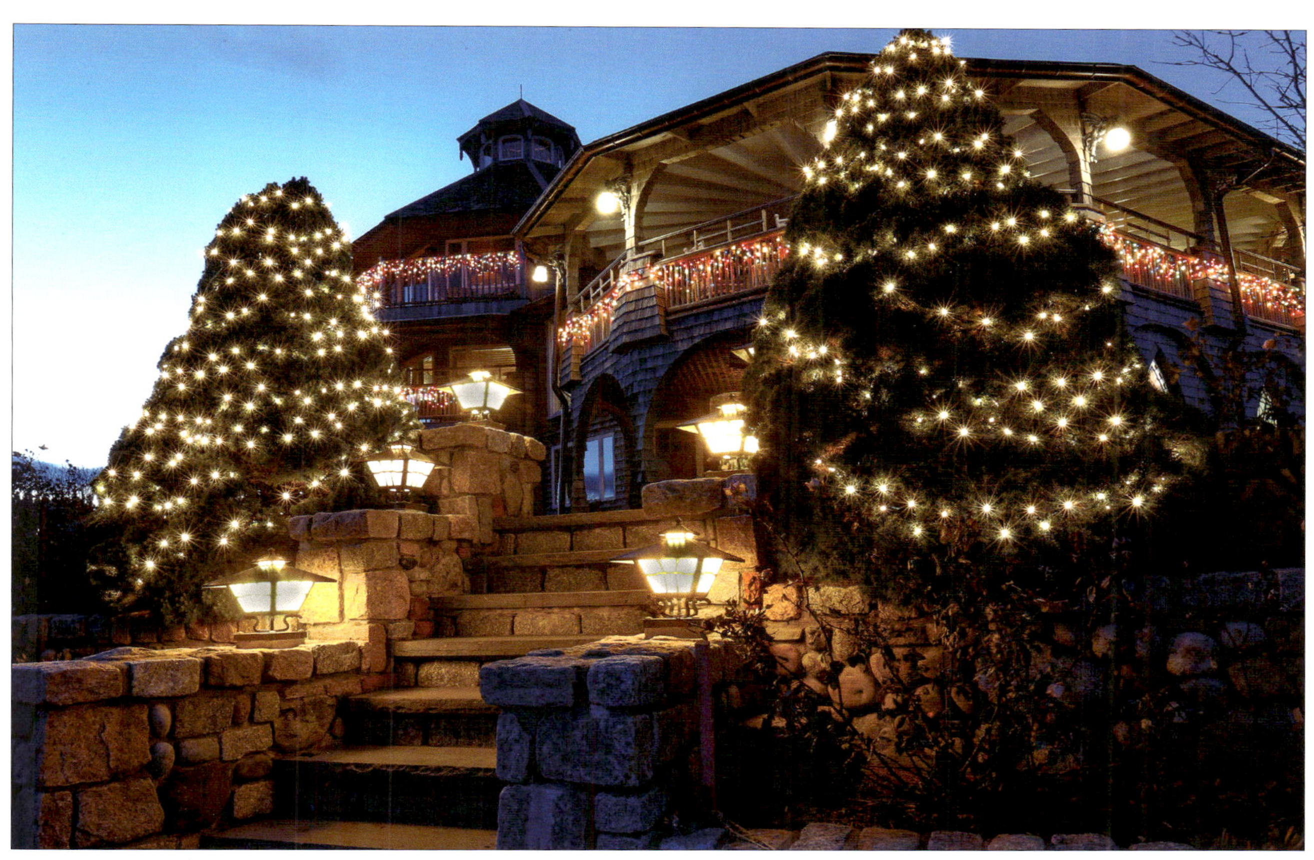

Steps coming up from Commercial Street decorated for the holidays, 2013

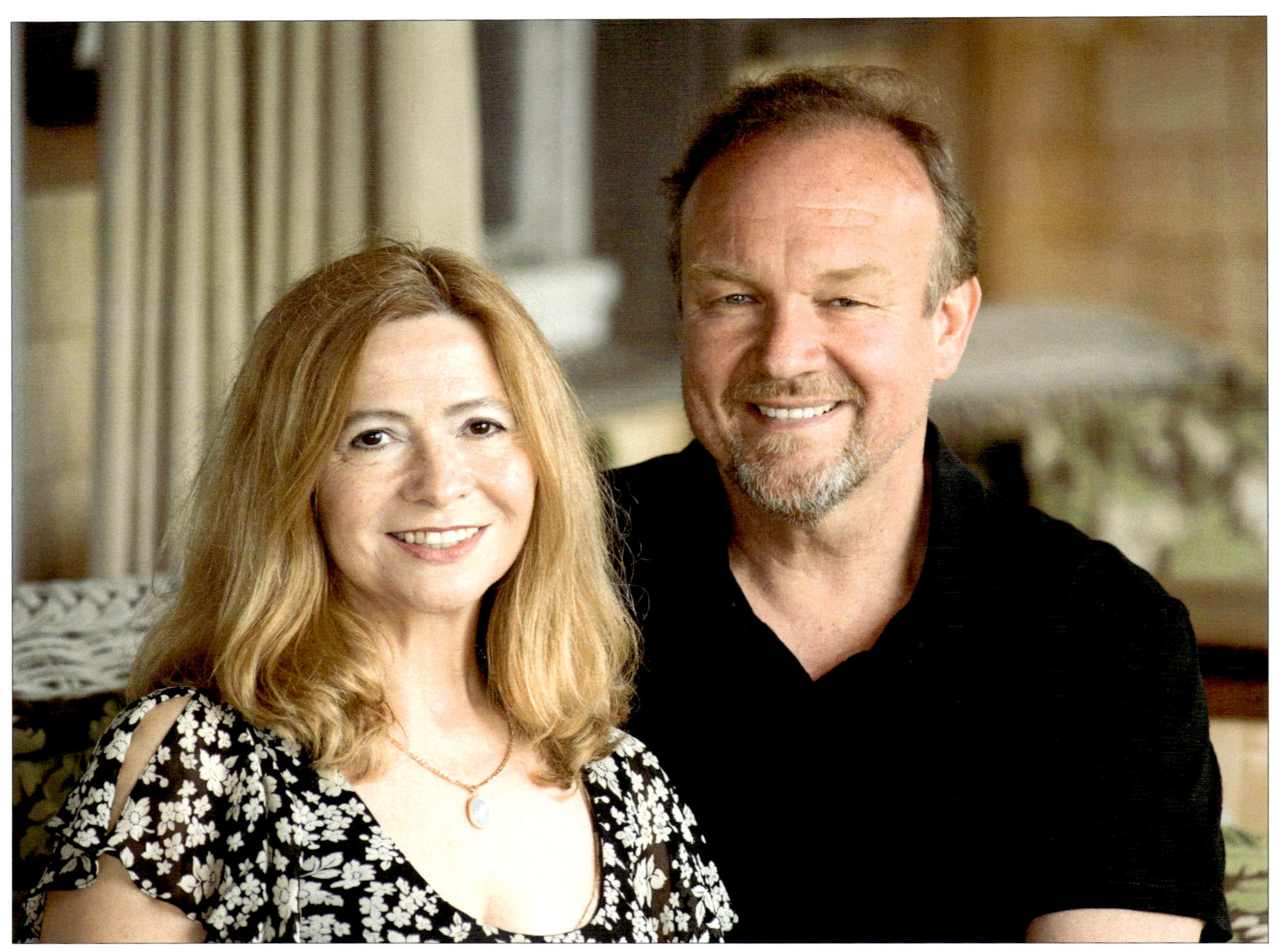

Eva and Stan Sikorski, who owned the inn from 2012 to 2022

I explained to Stan and Eva that you will own this on paper, but you really don't own it at all. You're really just caretakers for the next people.

They embrace and embody the Land's End Inn tradition of creating an atmosphere where people will start talking to each other and share ideas.

- Michael MacIntyre

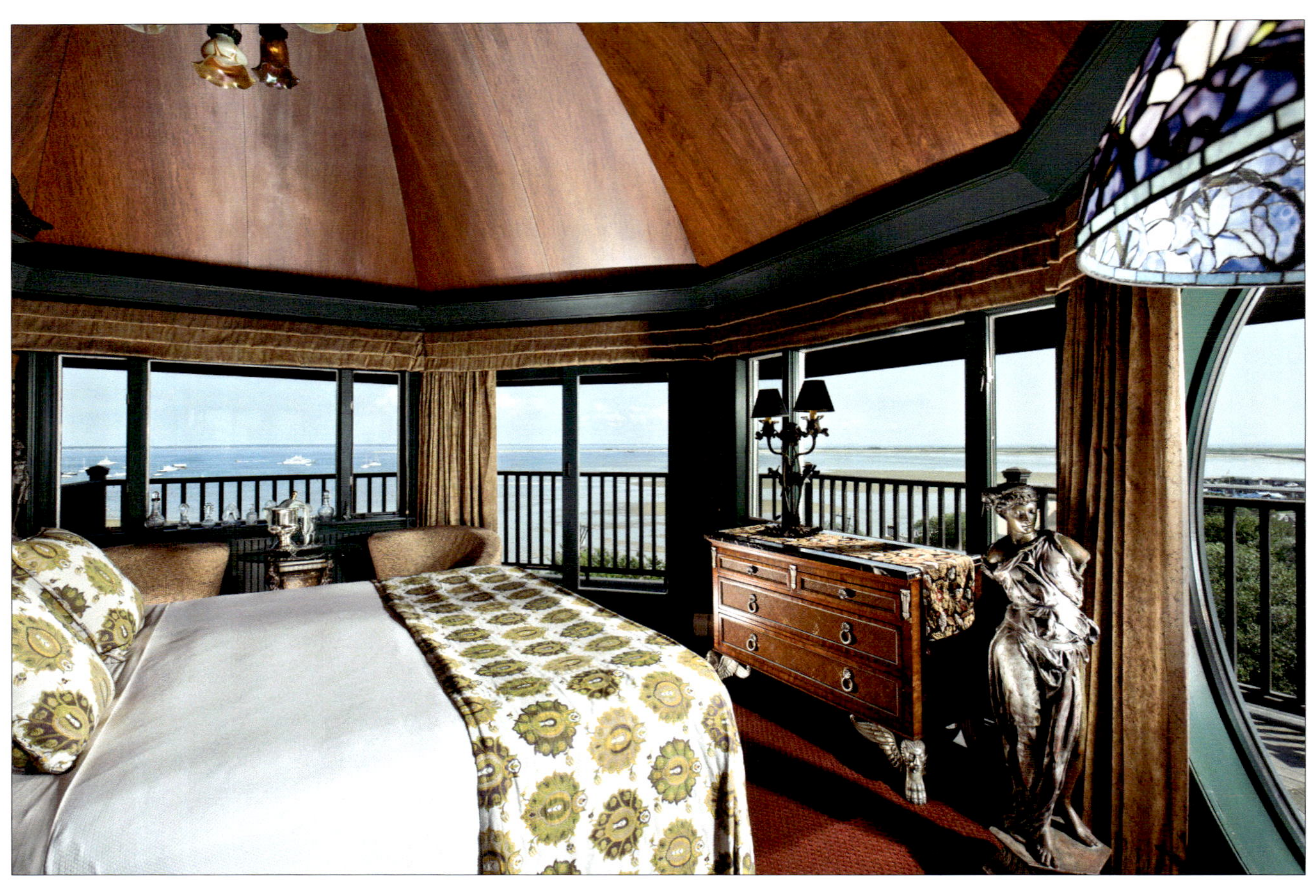

Bay Tower Room, 2017

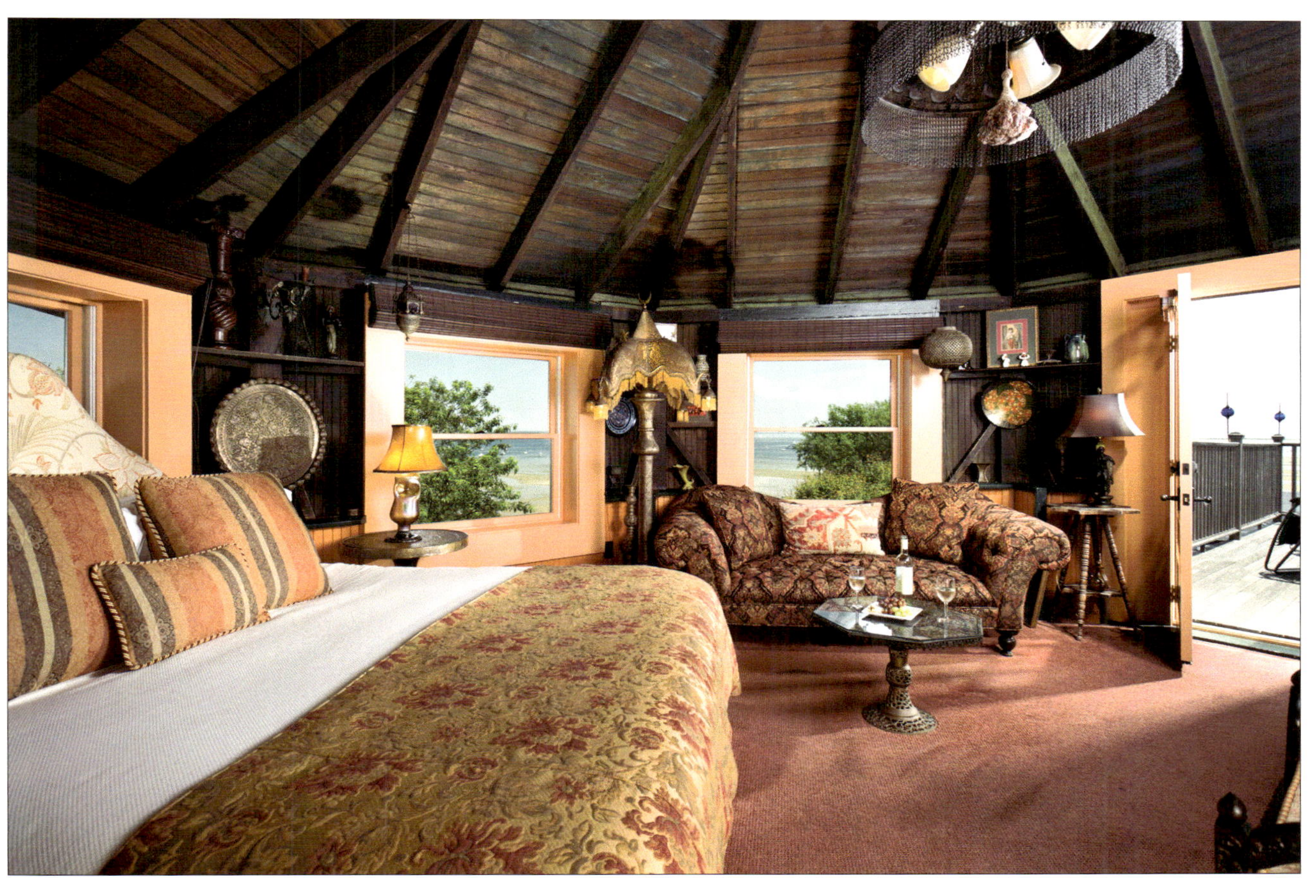

Moroccan Tower Room, 2017

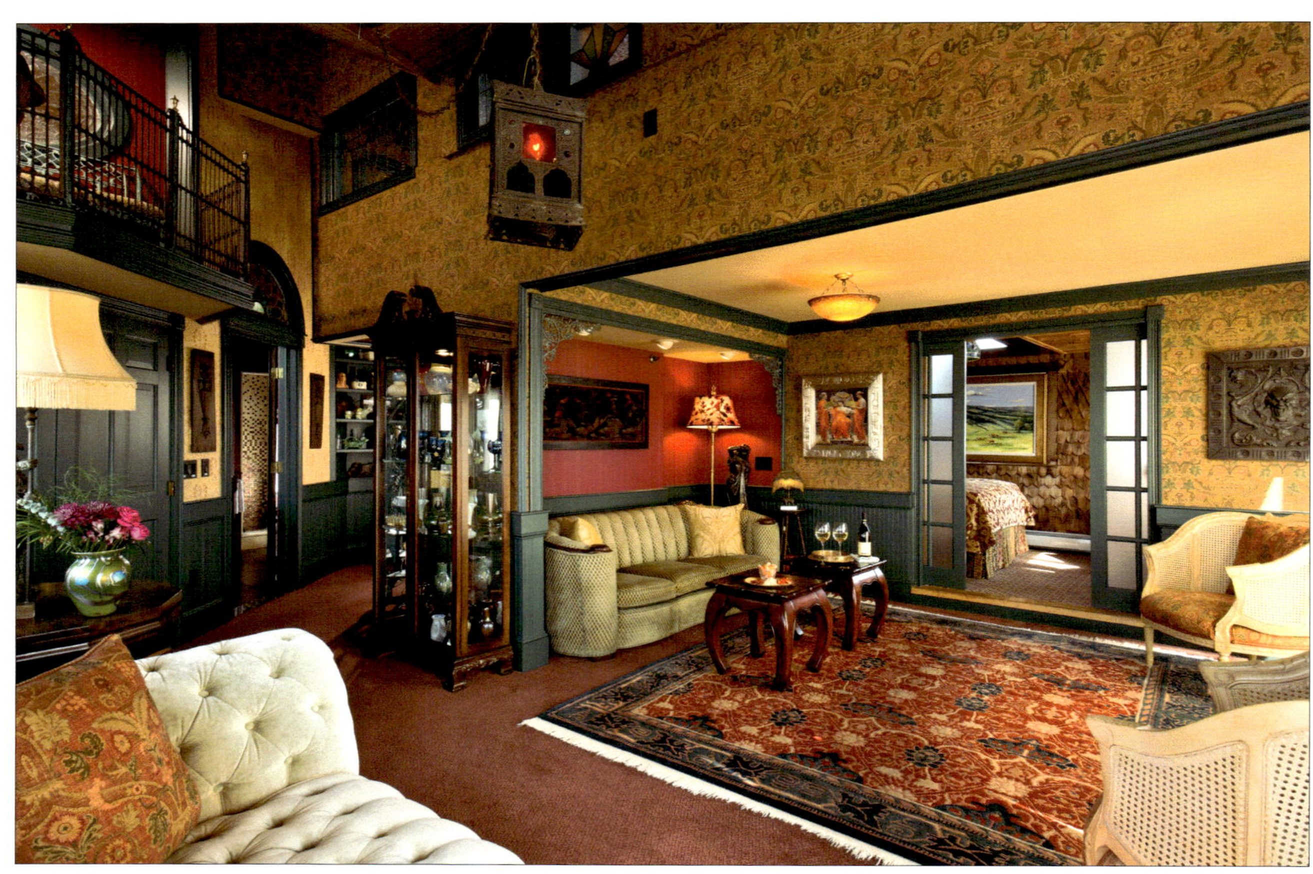

Schoolman Suite, 2013. Note the inaccessible balcony, another example of David Schoolman's whimsy, in the upper left.

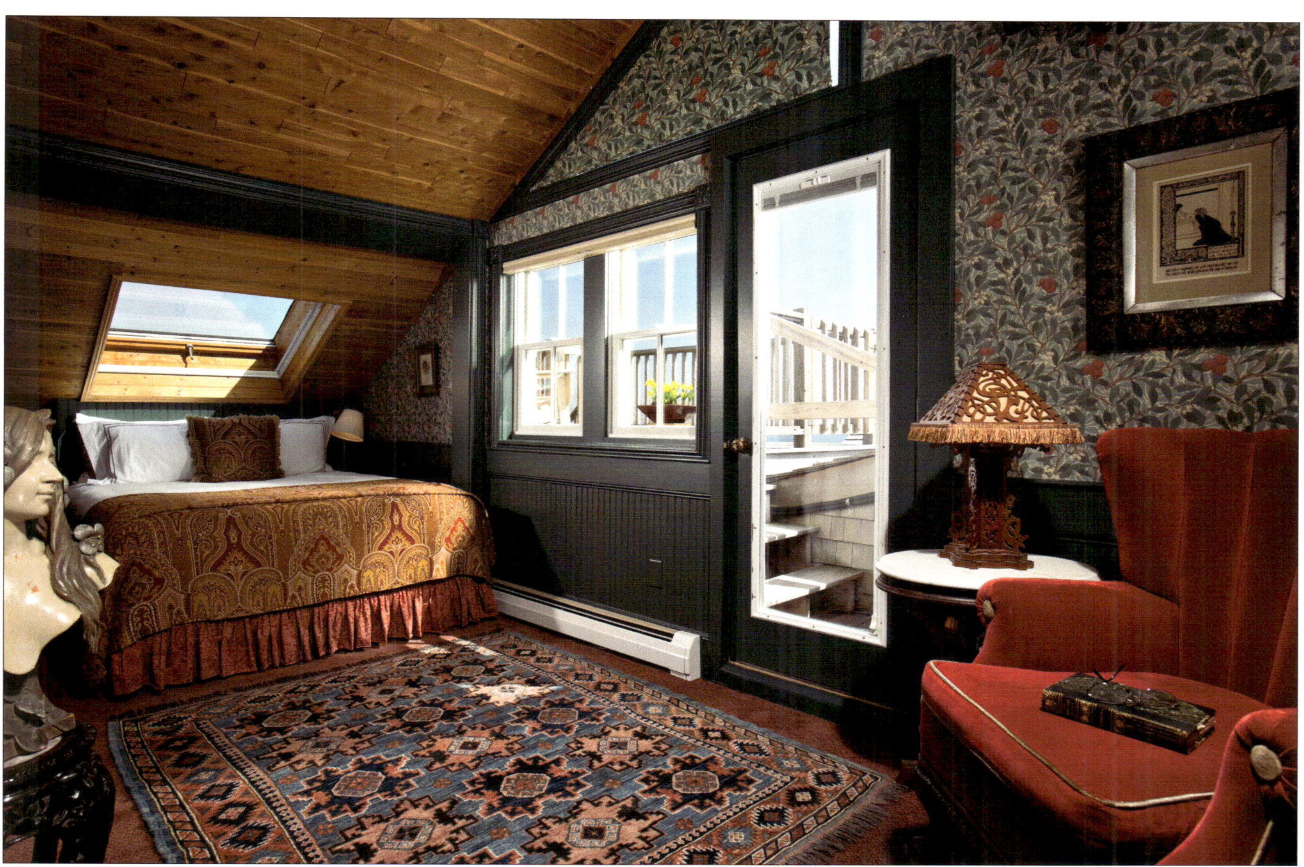

Higgins Room, 2013

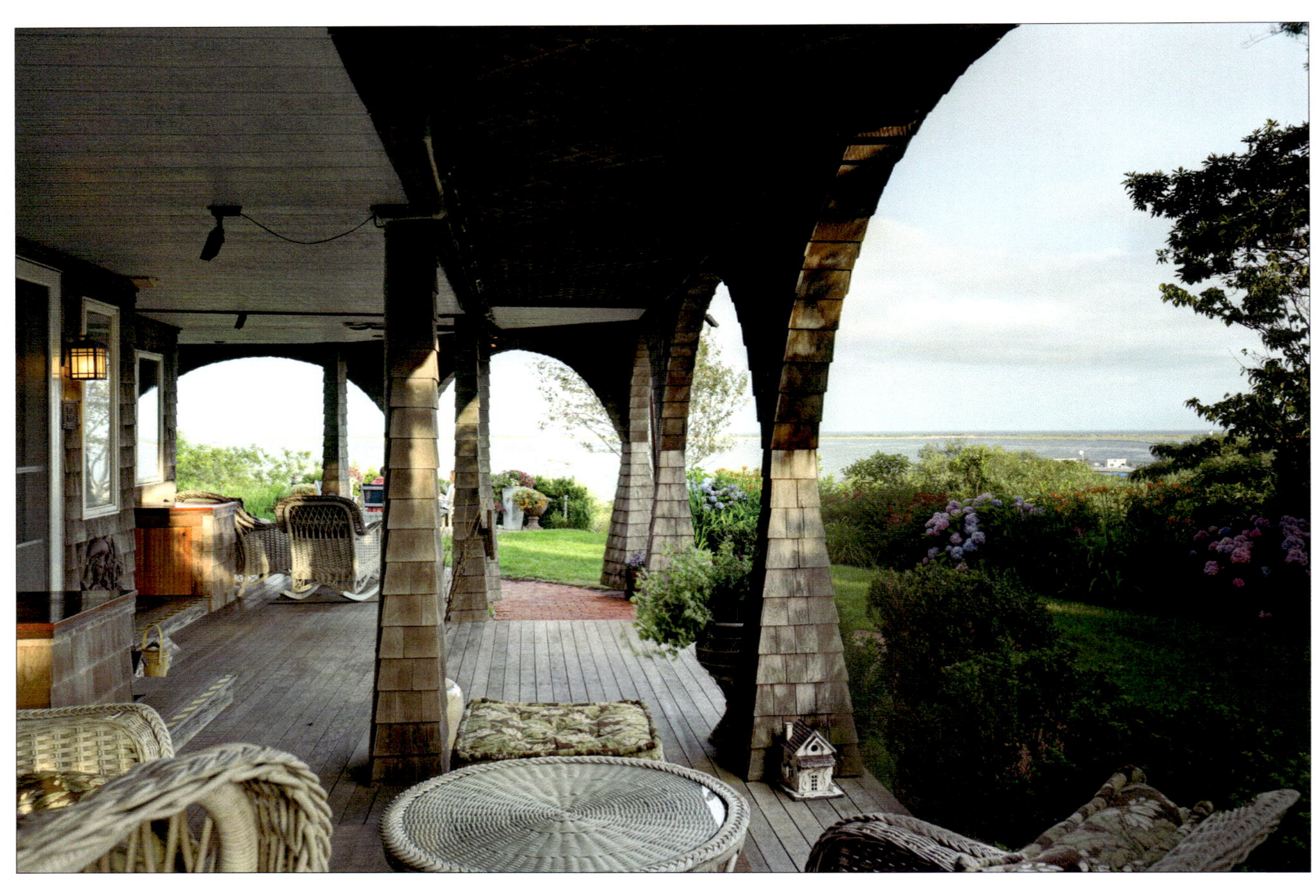

View from veranda off the West Indies Room, 2017

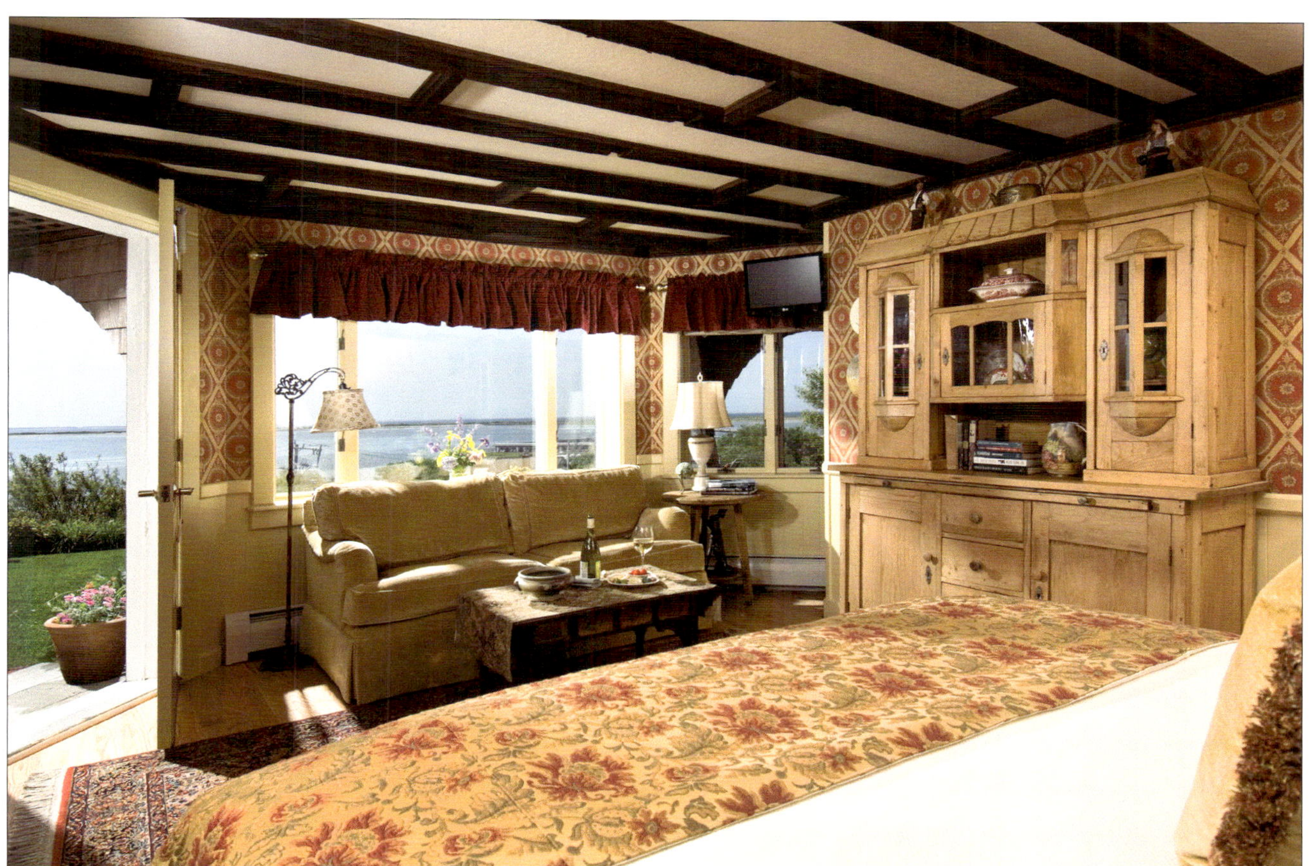

English Garden Room, 2011

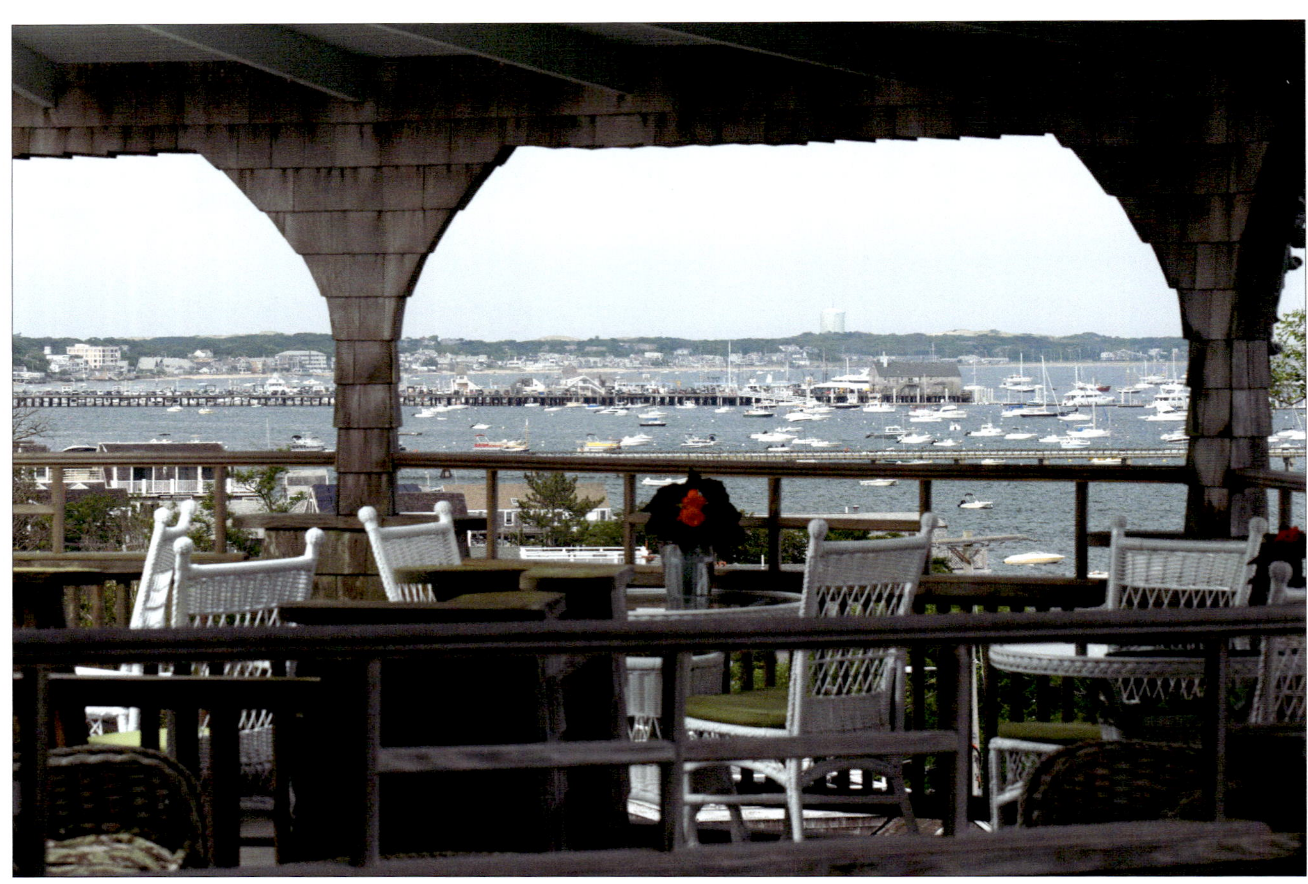

View of Provincetown Harbor from veranda, 2017

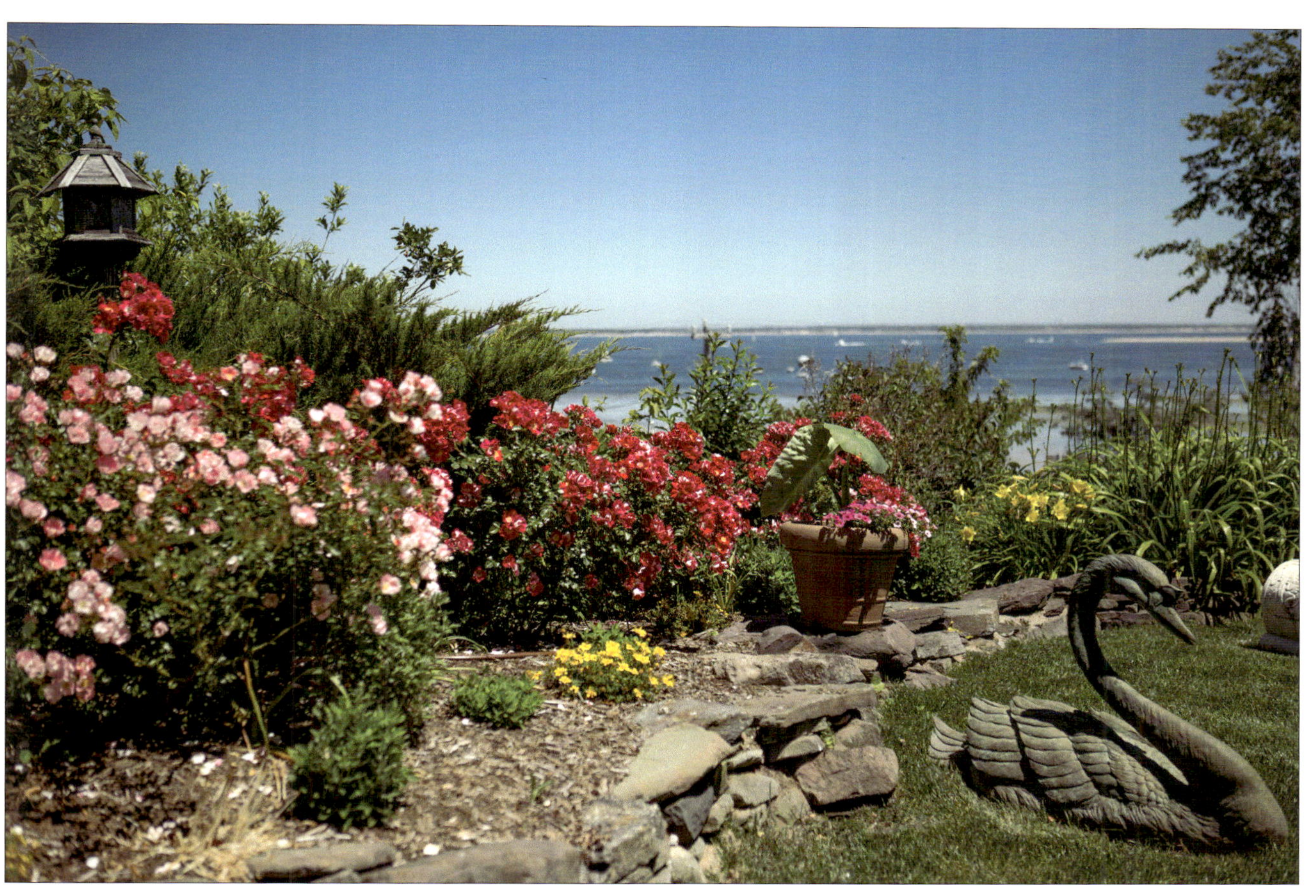

Gardens, 2016

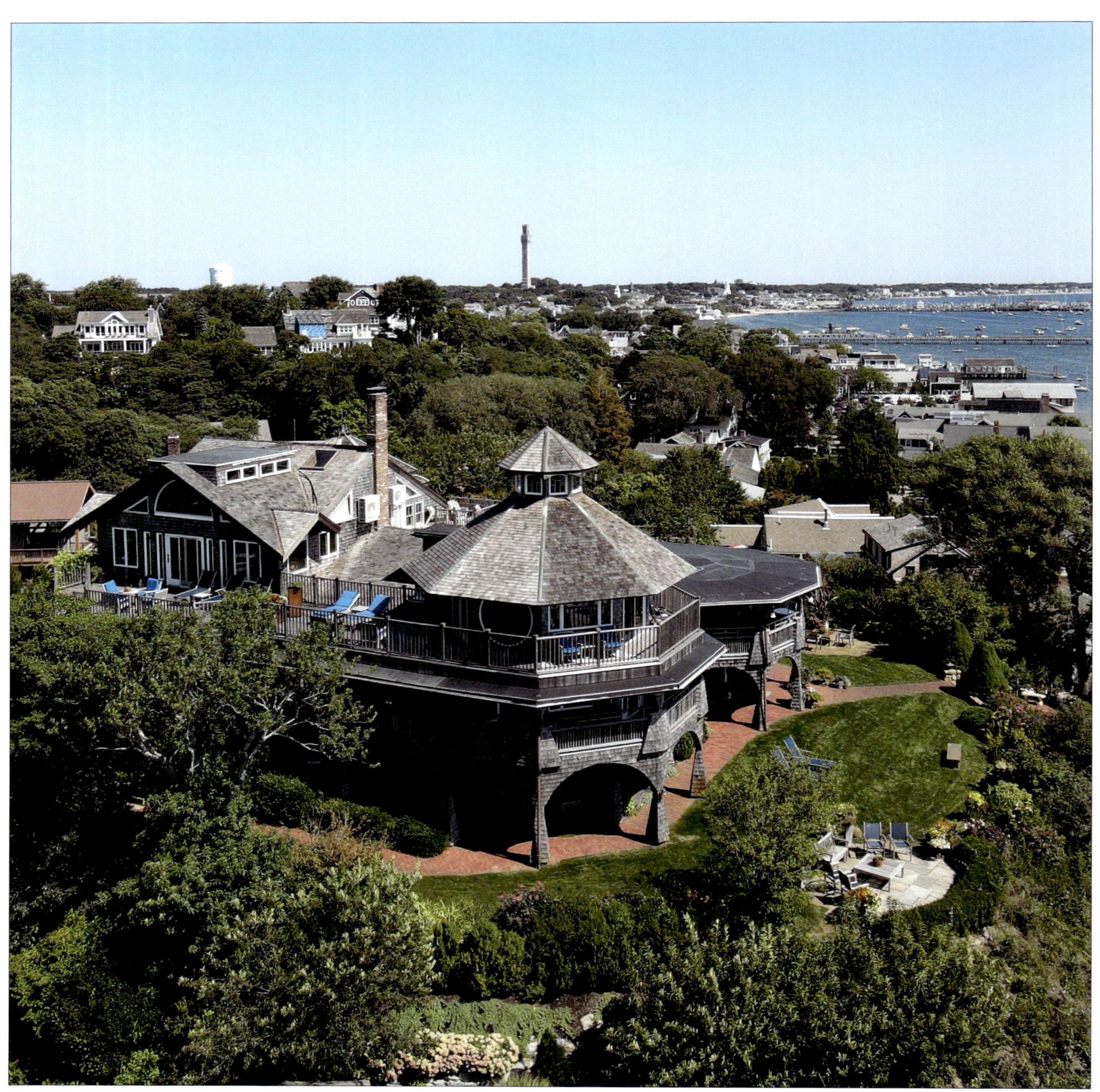

Land's End Inn, with Provincetown Monument in background, 2021

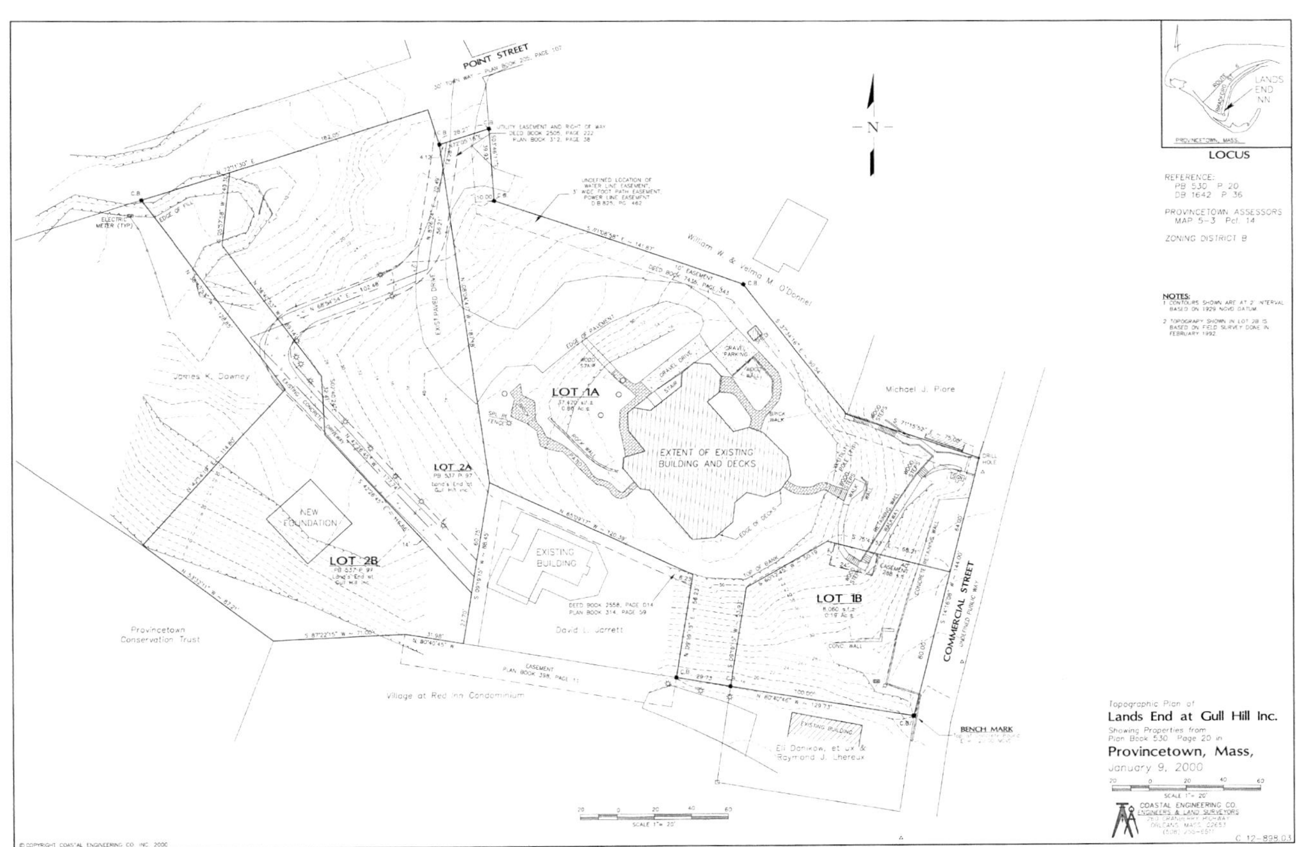

Most recent topographic survey of Land's End Inn, 2000

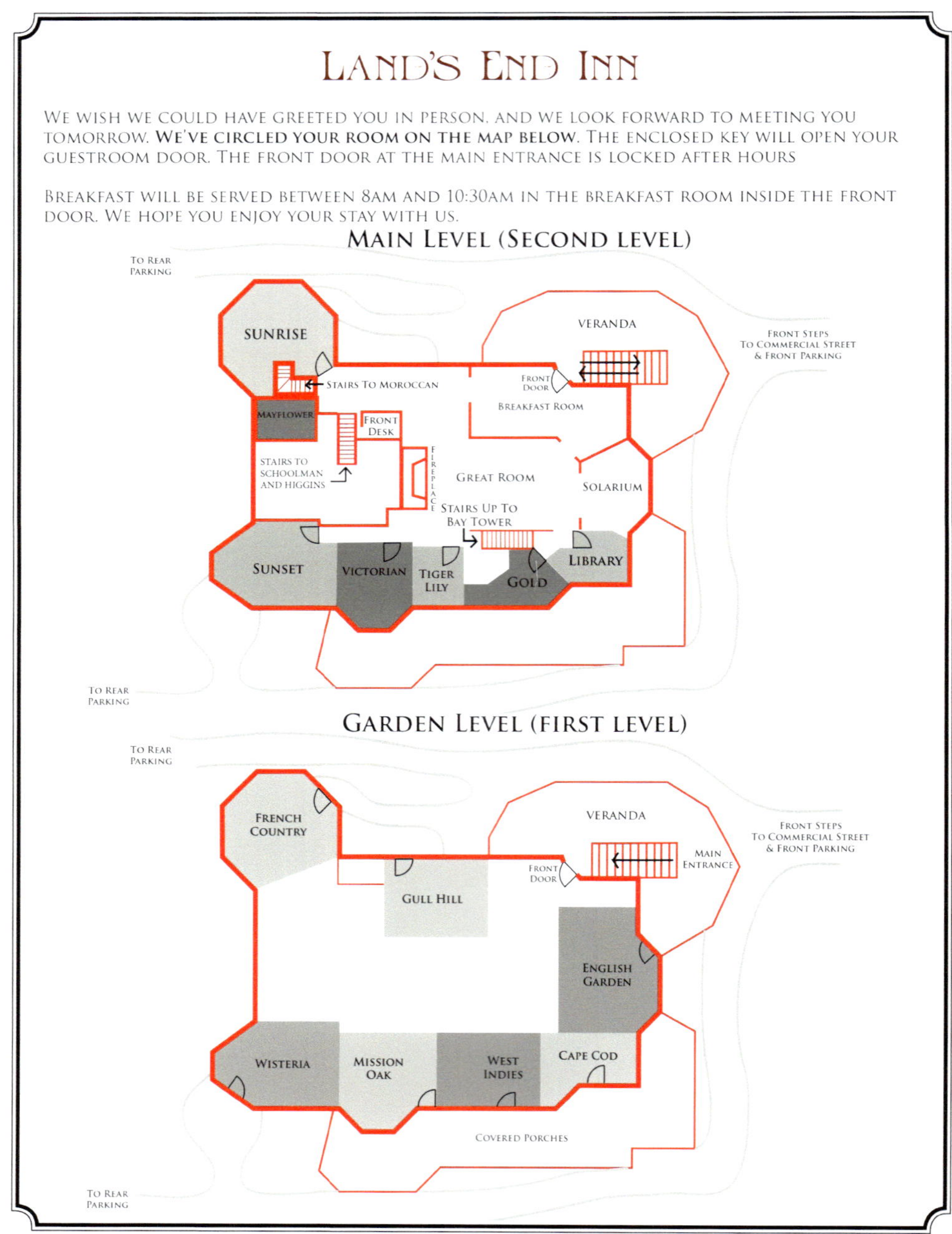

Maps used to guide guests arriving late to their rooms, 2021

LAND'S END INN

TOWER LEVEL (THIRD LEVEL)

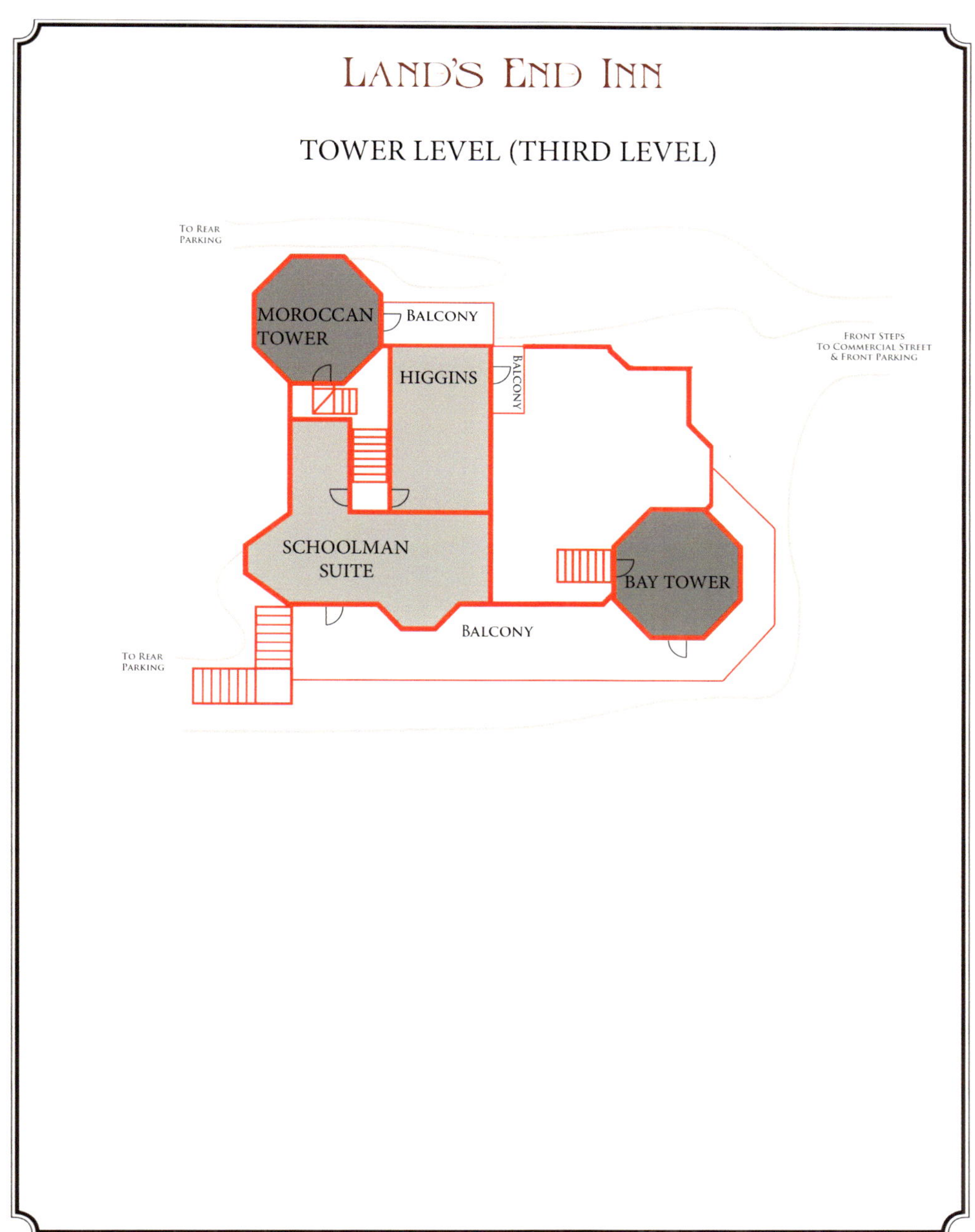

Maps used to guide guests arriving late to their rooms, 2021

Trevor and Ed… The Art of Evolution

In 2022, we bought the inn from the Sikorskis to preserve and enhance its place in the community. We immediately brought in good friend and hospitality maestro Peter Sullivan, also a year-round resident of Provincetown, as general manager. One of our first moves was to restore the inn's logo to one inspired by a sign created by David Schoolman. The existing moniker on Commercial Street was quickly replaced with a whimsical pink, purple, and gold sign that beckoned all who walked by to make the climb up Gull Hill and explore the inn. In the spirit of incorporating the work of local artists, we brought in stone craftsman Frankie Rice, a native of neighboring Truro, to build a firepit on the lawn. We also expanded the inn's program of welcoming local charities to the property for fundraisers.

Like the previous generations of stewards looking after the inn, we are committed to preserving its history, building on its legacy, offering an outstanding guest experience, and maintaining strong ties with the local community. Similar to David Schoolman, we created a nonprofit organization, the Land's End Foundation, to which the inn will pass after our lifetimes. We chartered the foundation to operate the inn as such for the enjoyment of all and to support the local arts and LGBTQ+ communities and allies for generations to come.

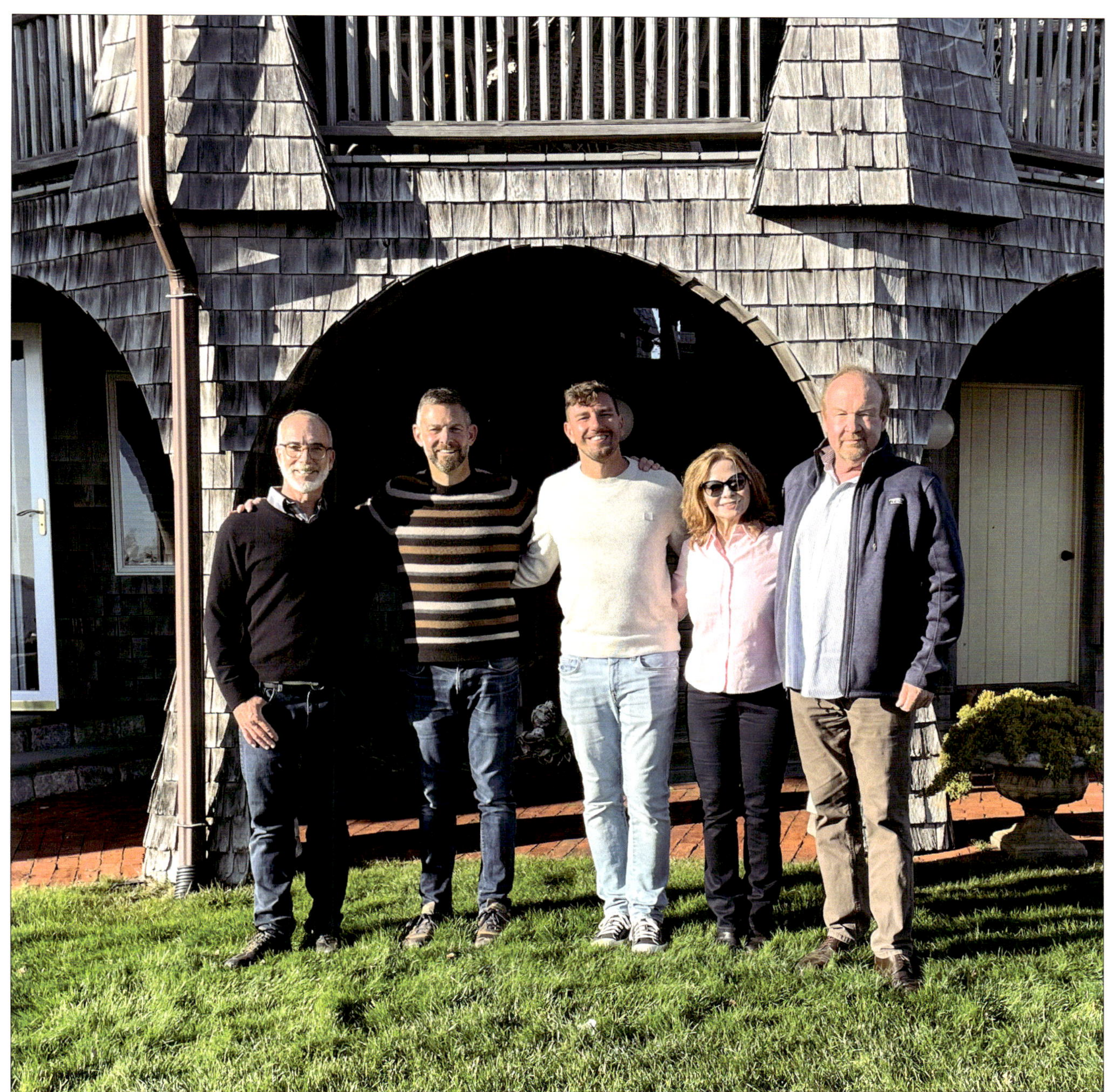

From left, Peter Sullivan, Ed Macri, Trevor Mikula, Eva Sikorski, and Stan Sikorski, 2021

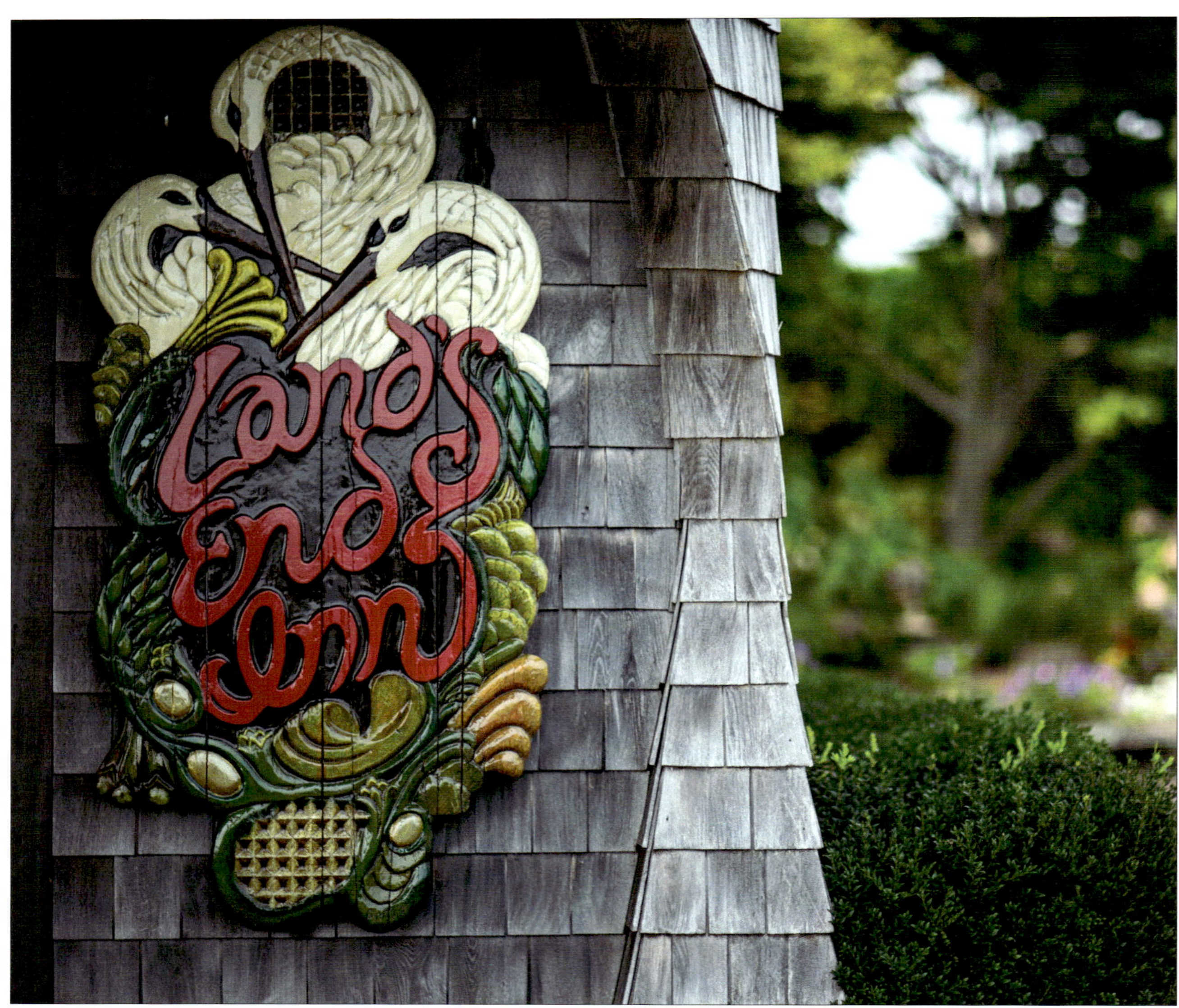

Sign from David Schoolman's era that inspired the update to the Land's End Inn logo, 2022

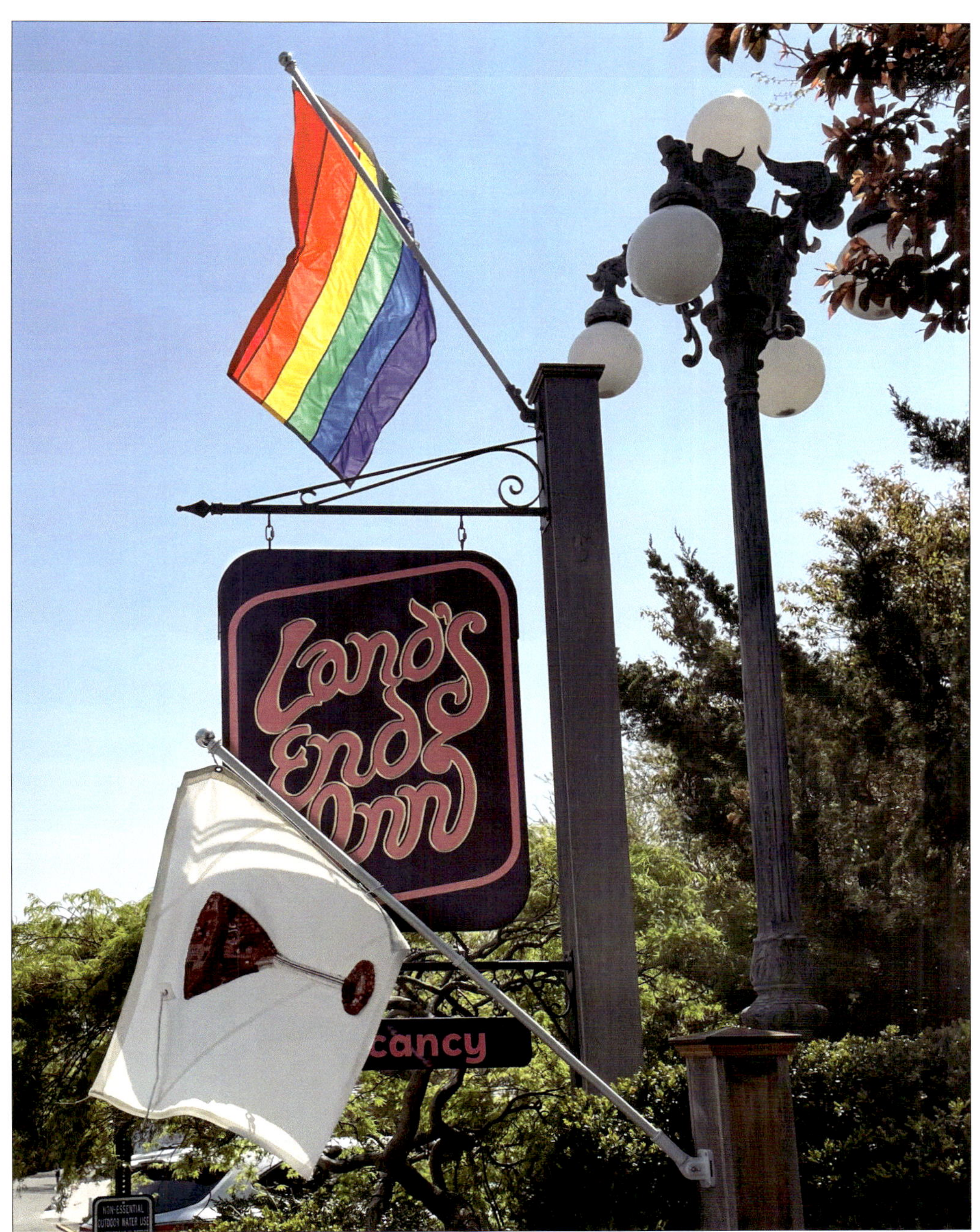

New sign on Commercial Street, 2023

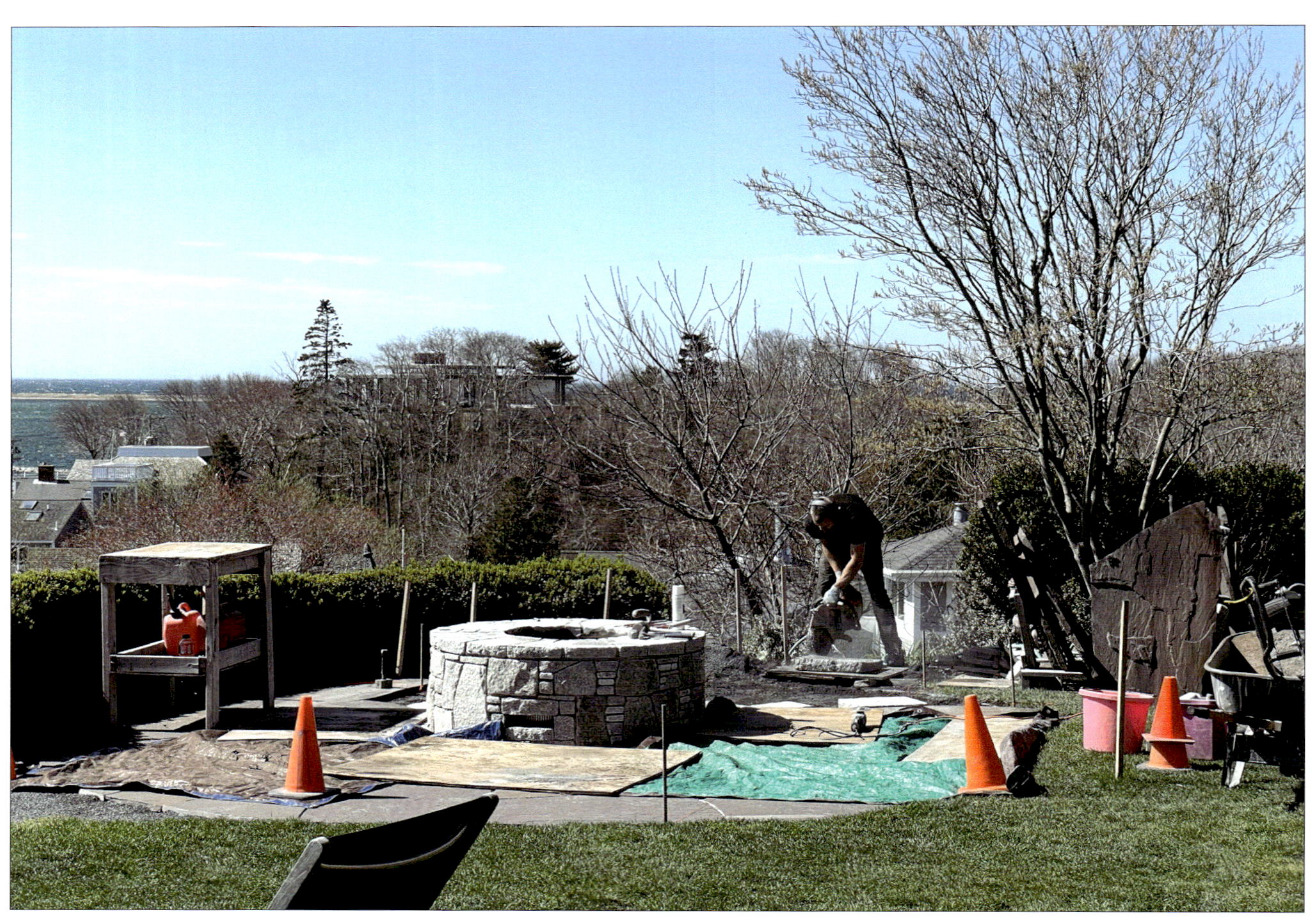

Construction of new firepit by local artisan Frankie Rice, 2023

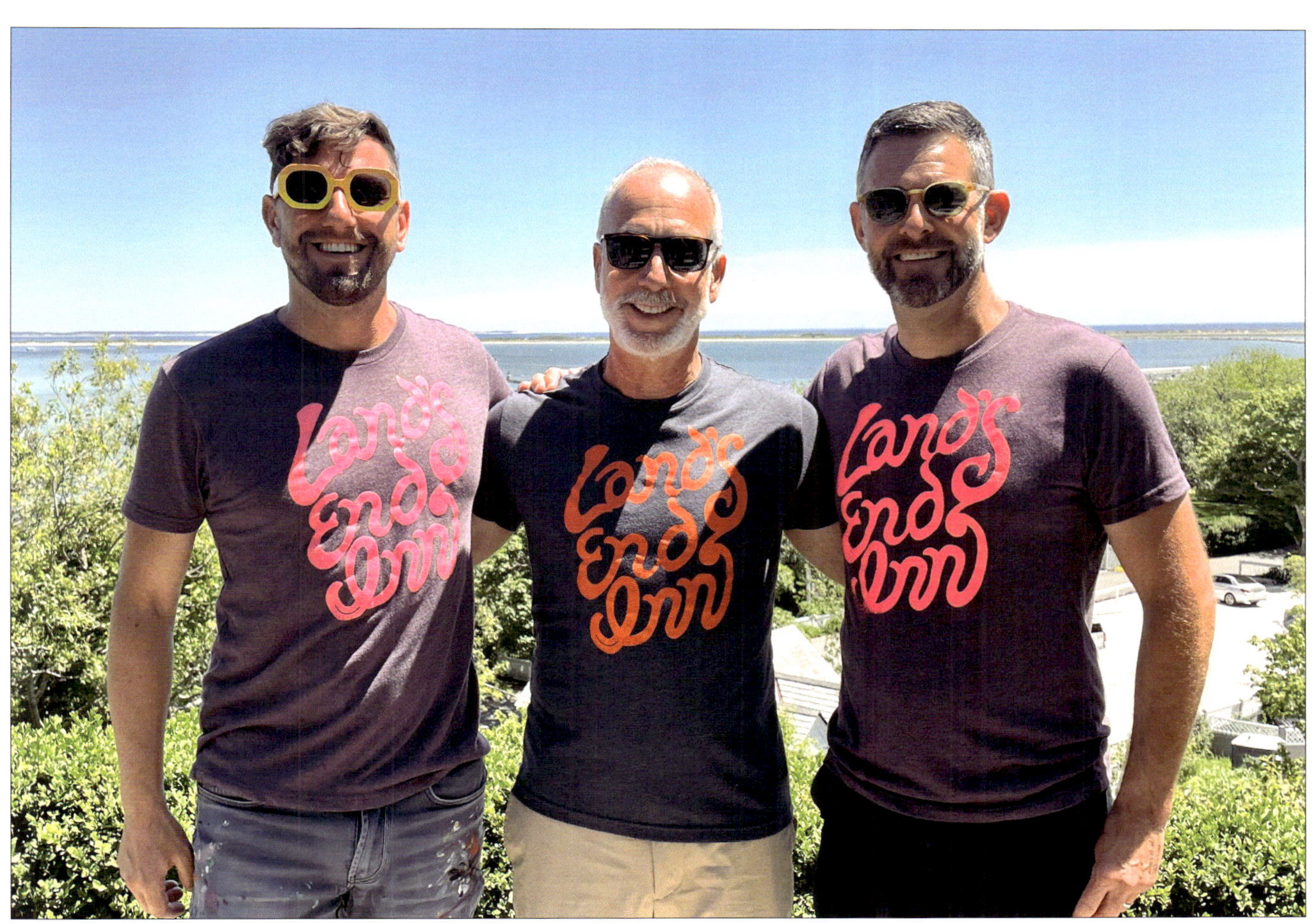

From left, Trevor Mikula, Peter Sullivan, and Ed Macri wearing the "new" classic logo T-shirts, 2022

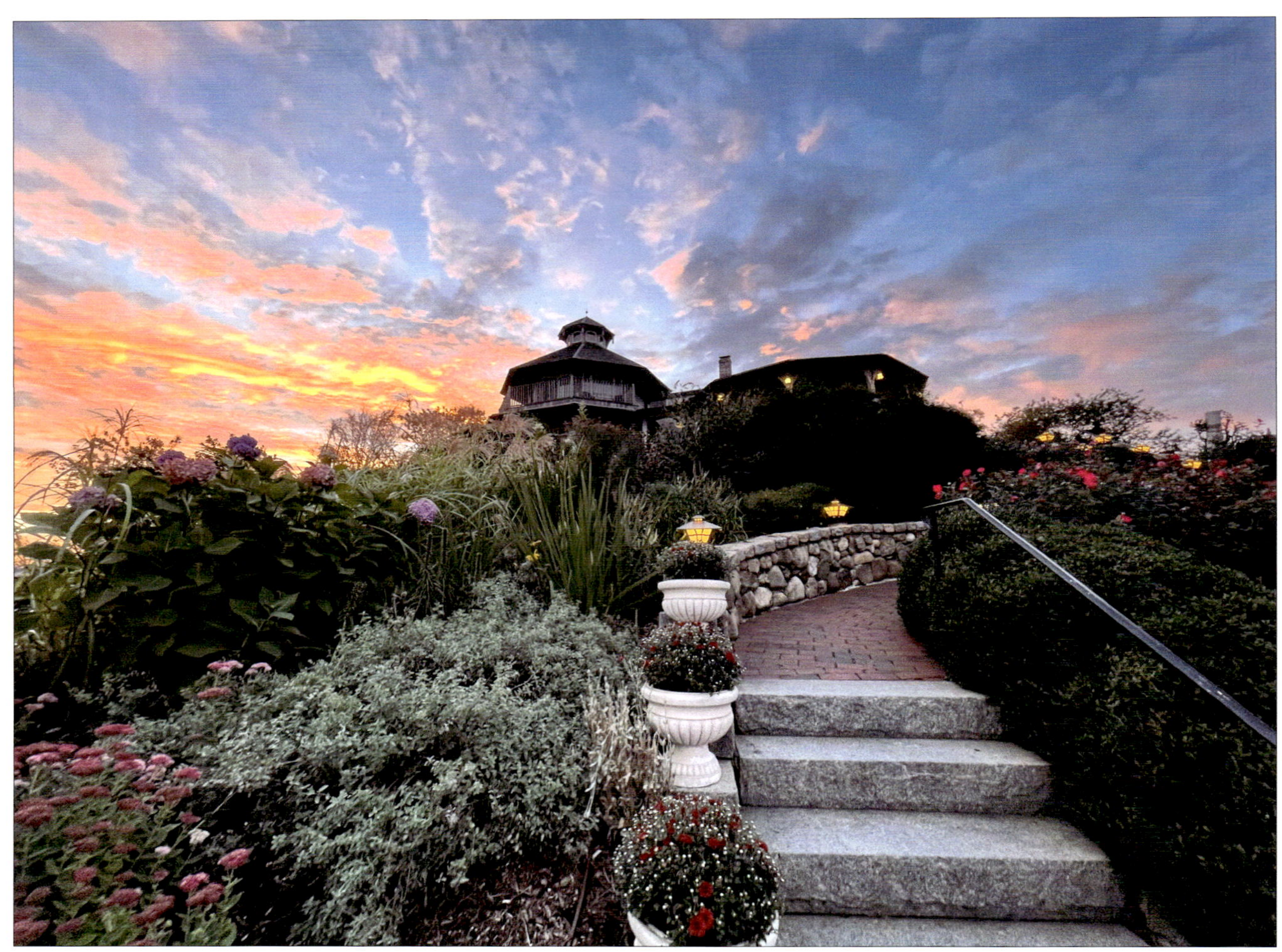

Pathway up to Land's End Inn, 2022

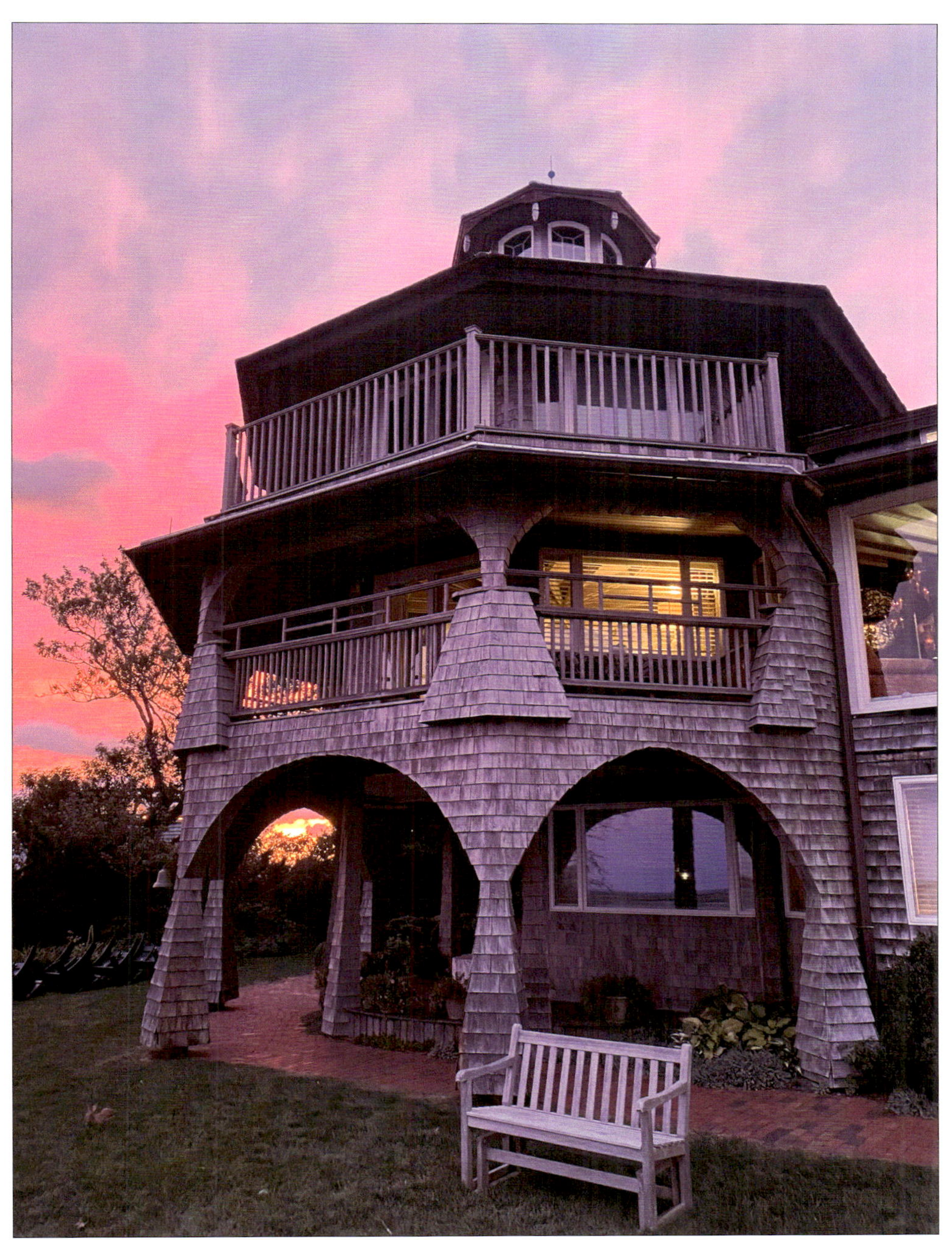

Sunset behind Land's End Inn, 2022

Chalice... Drink in the View

In 2023, to build on the inn's legacy as a community hub in Provincetown's West End, we opened Chalice as a gathering place, offering wine and beer on the lawn on summer afternoons—a throwback to David Schoolman's parties.

The logo for Chalice was inspired by and in honor of Ed's prior partner Will Rowan and dear friend Rachel Scholow, both of whom had passed in recent years. Will and Rachel were the best of friends and joyful inspirations to all who knew them. They shared a house in Provincetown's East End with other local hospitality workers. Whenever they were throwing a party, they hung a chalice flag on the street in front of their house—a call that all were welcome and fun was to be had. Mike Miller, the owner of *Ptownie*, recreated the flag, and it hangs on Commercial Street whenever Chalice is open.

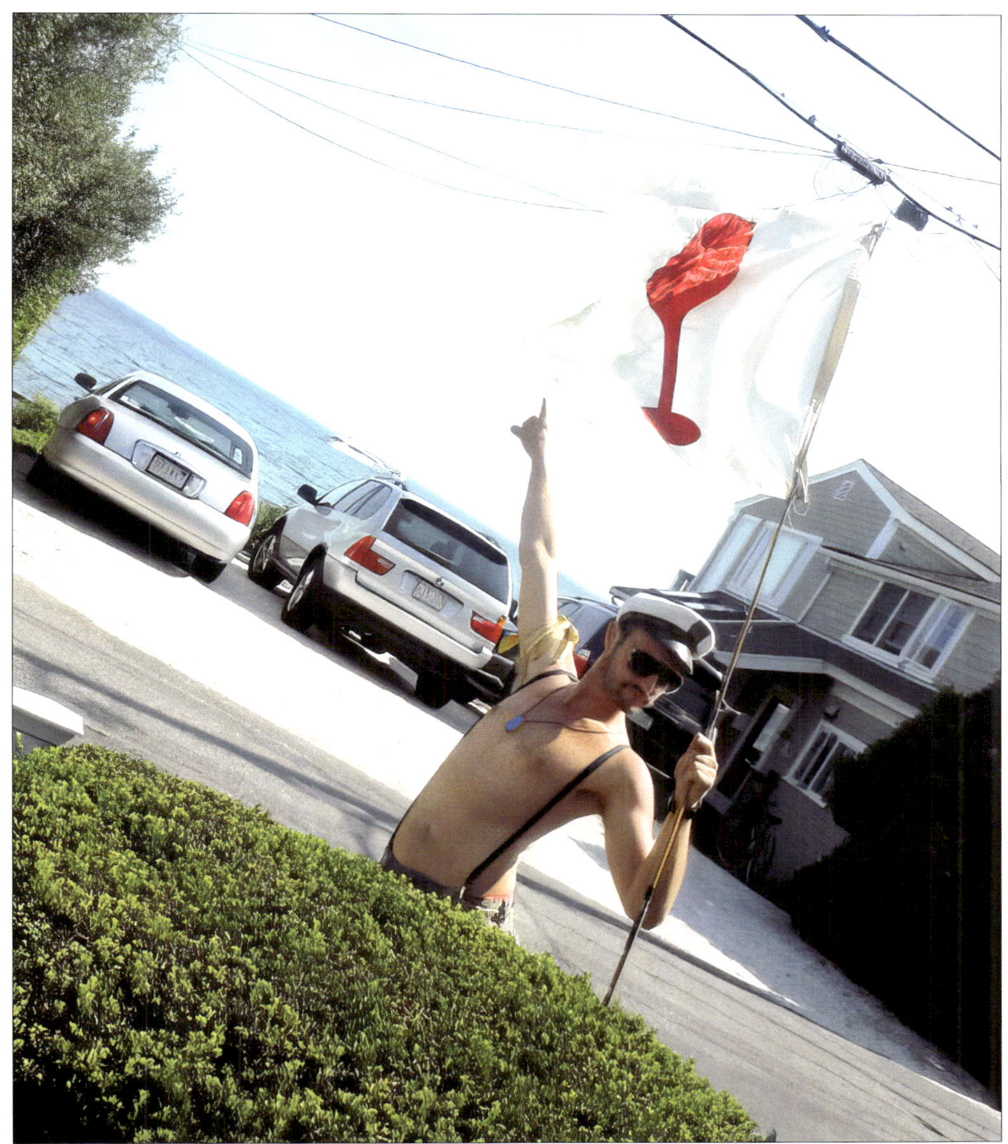

Will Rowan hoisting the flag that inspired Chalice to welcome passersby to a Provincetown Carnival house party in the East End, 2011

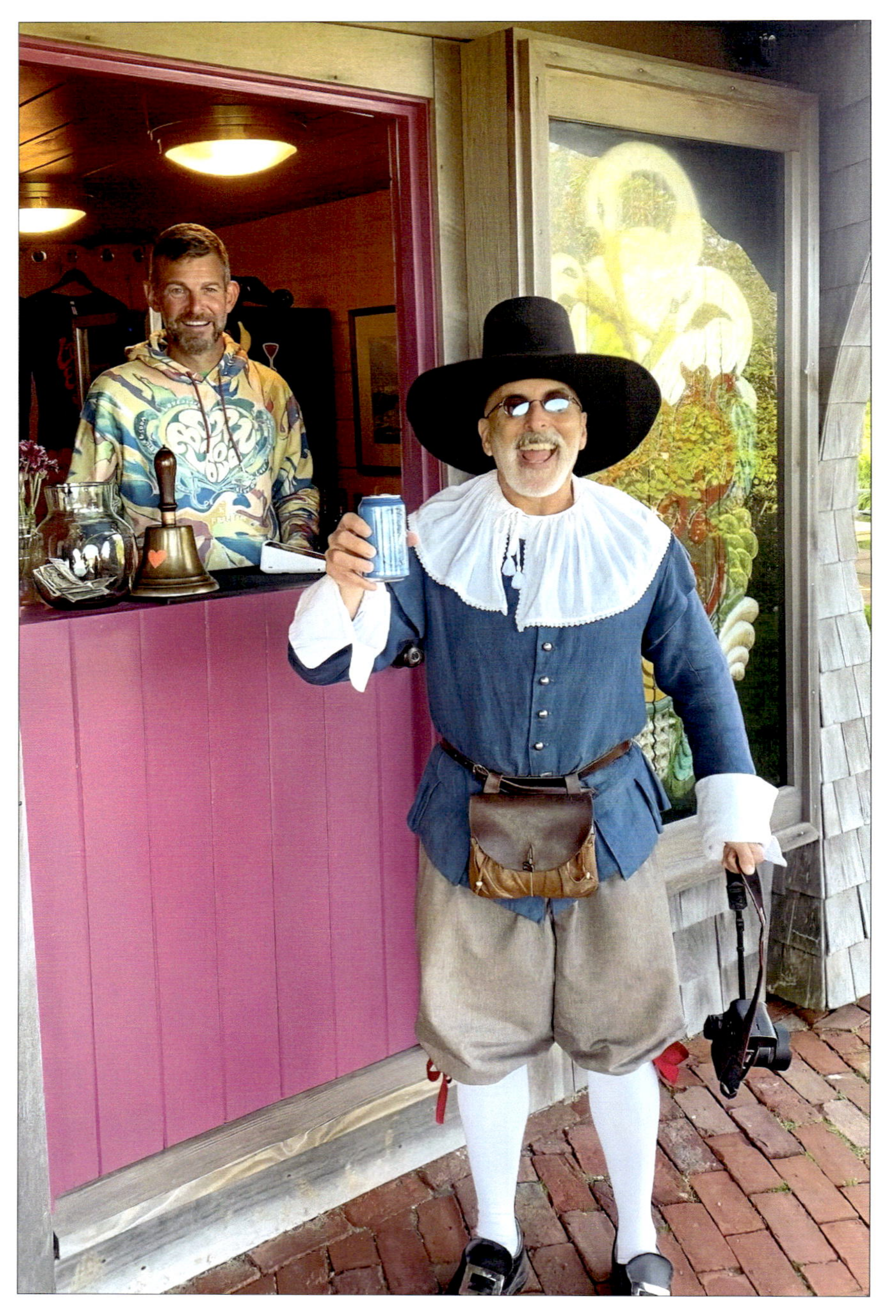

Ed Macri behind the bar serving Provincetown's town crier, 2023

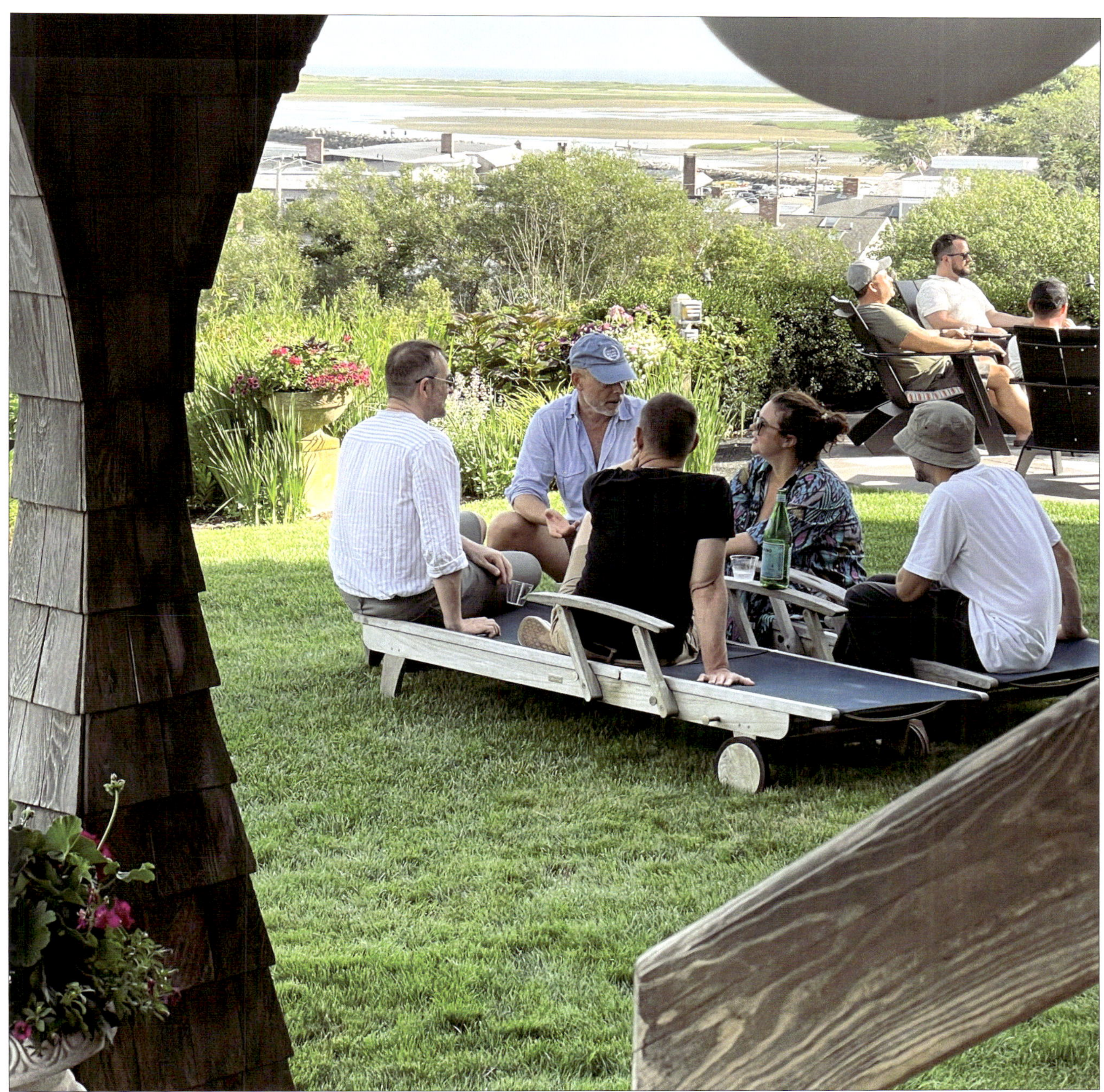

Provincetown locals gathering at Chalice, 2023

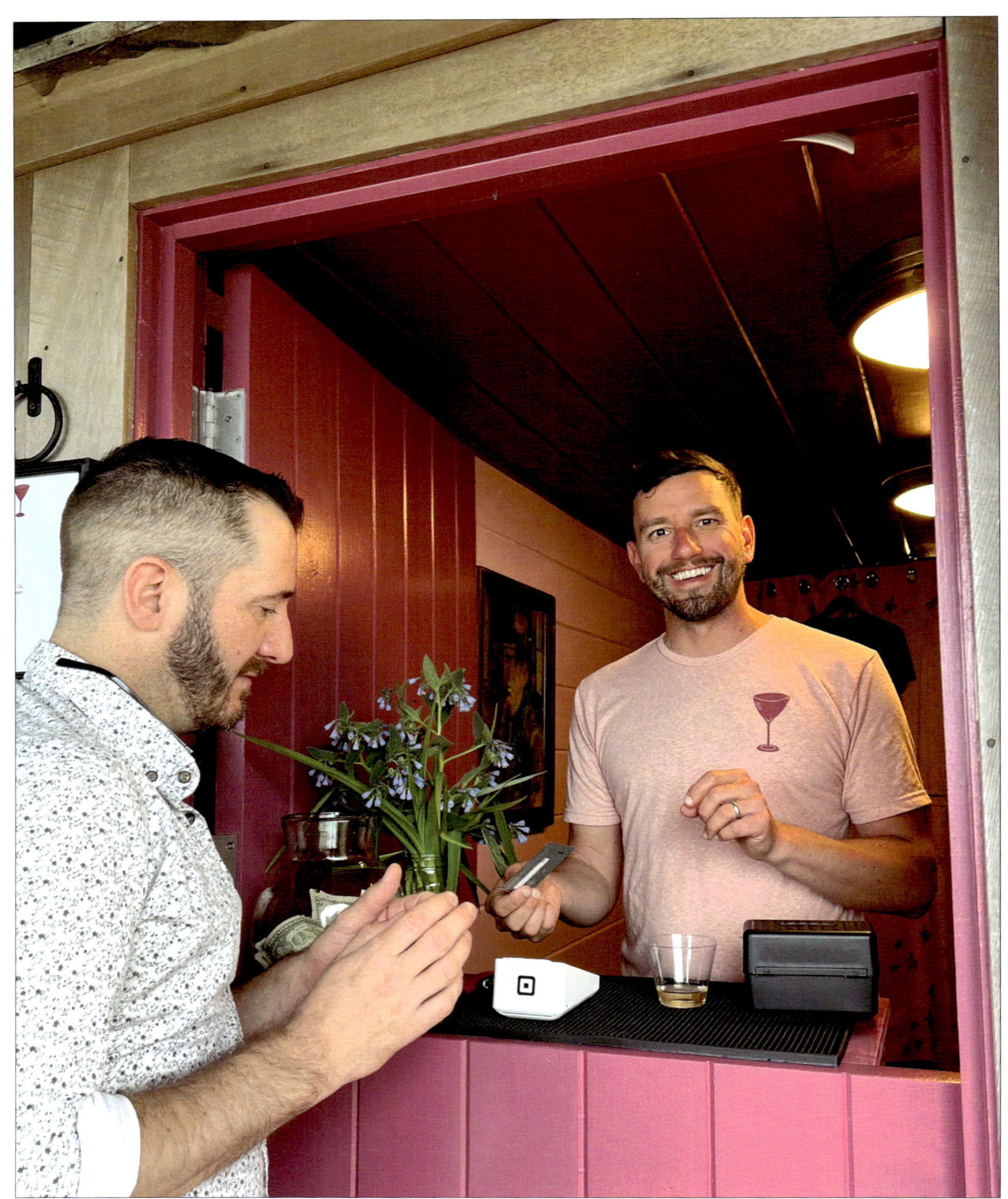

Trevor Mikula behind the bar at Chalice, 2023

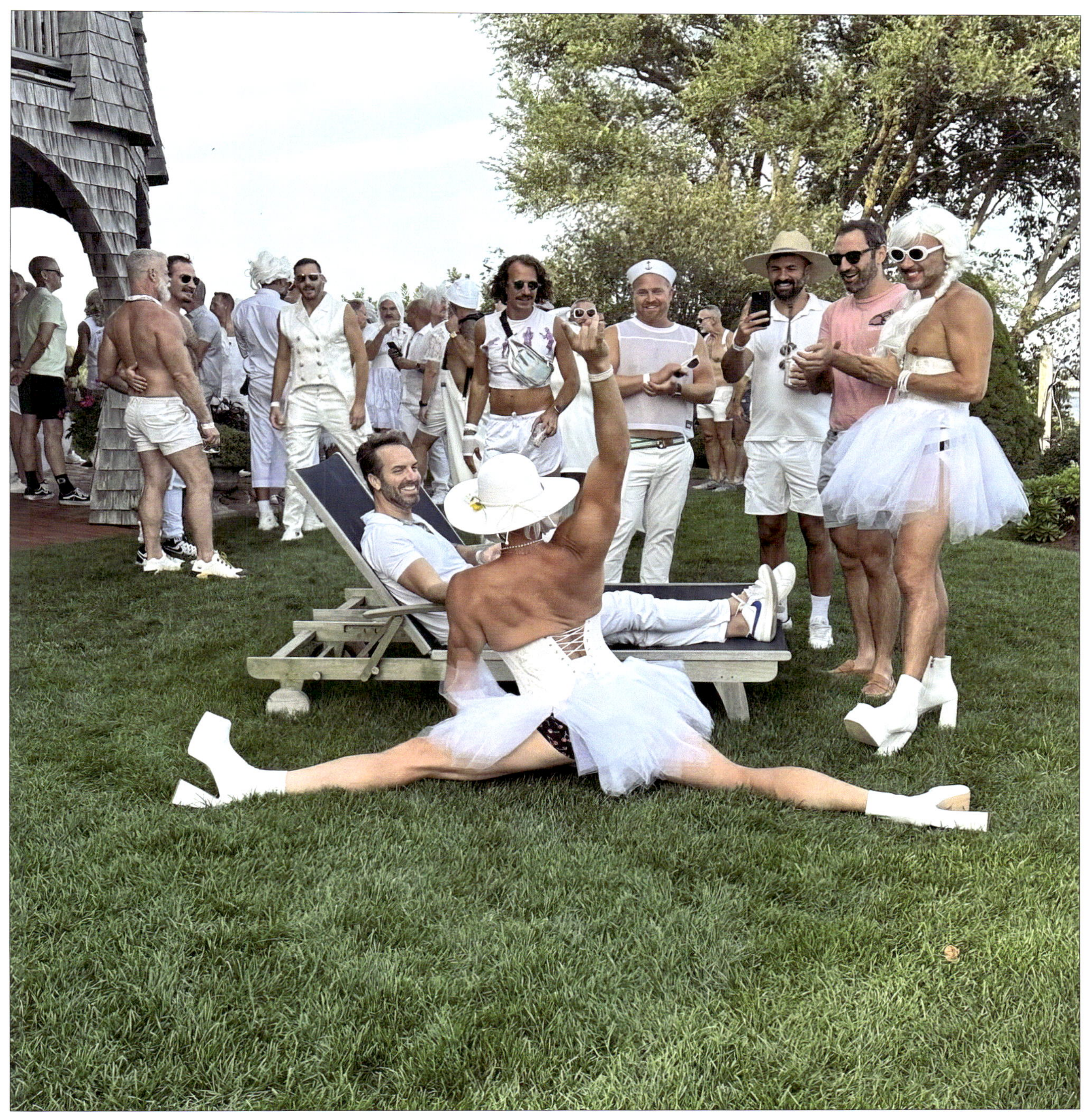

Guests at Chalice coming from Provincetown's annual White Party fundraiser for Outer Cape Health Services, 2023

Chalice is quintessential Provincetown—quirky and inclusive. It brings together townies and travelers to enjoy the most stunning views in town.

- Andy Towle, neighbor

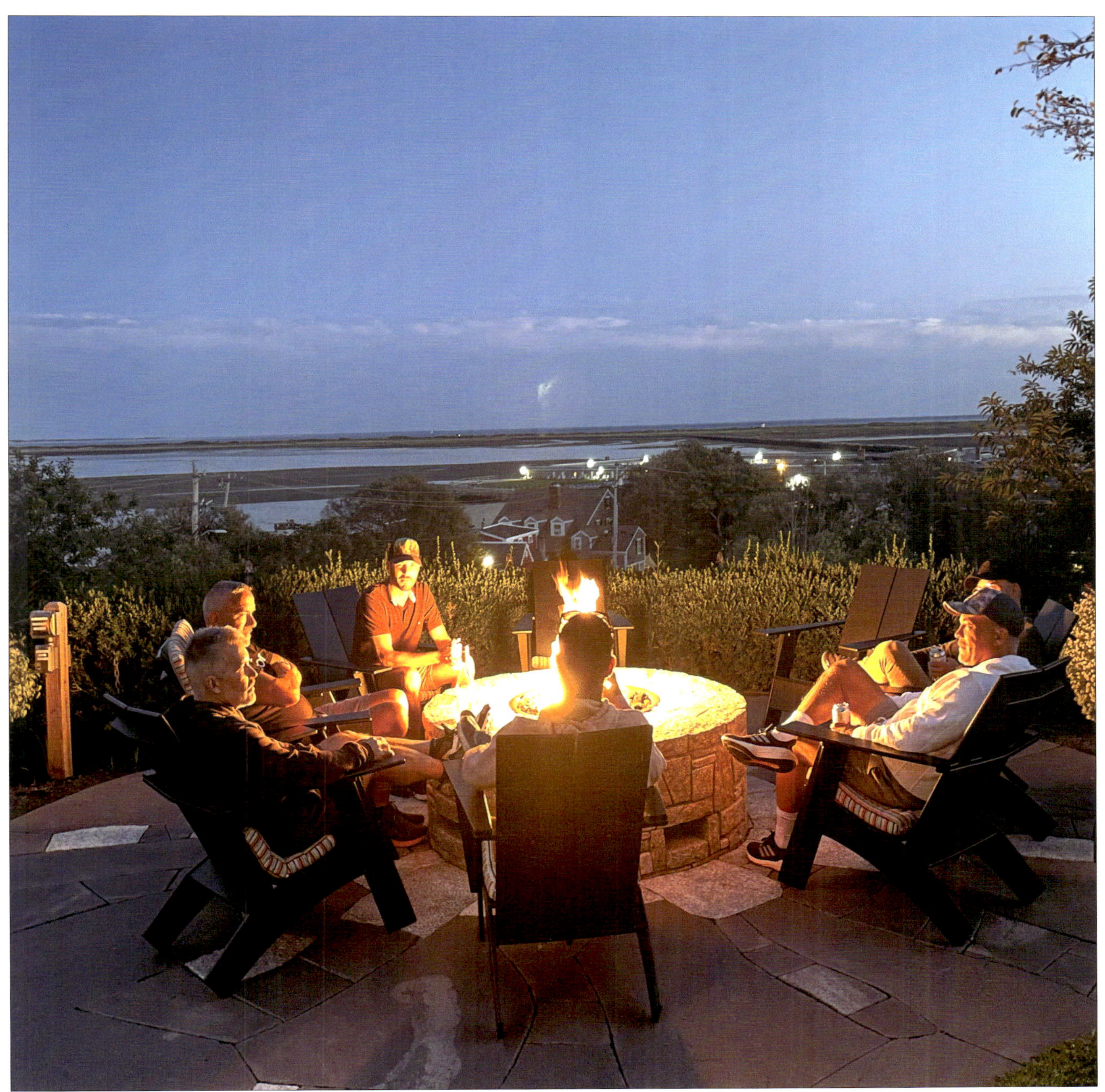

Neighbor Andy Towle and other Provincetown locals, 2023

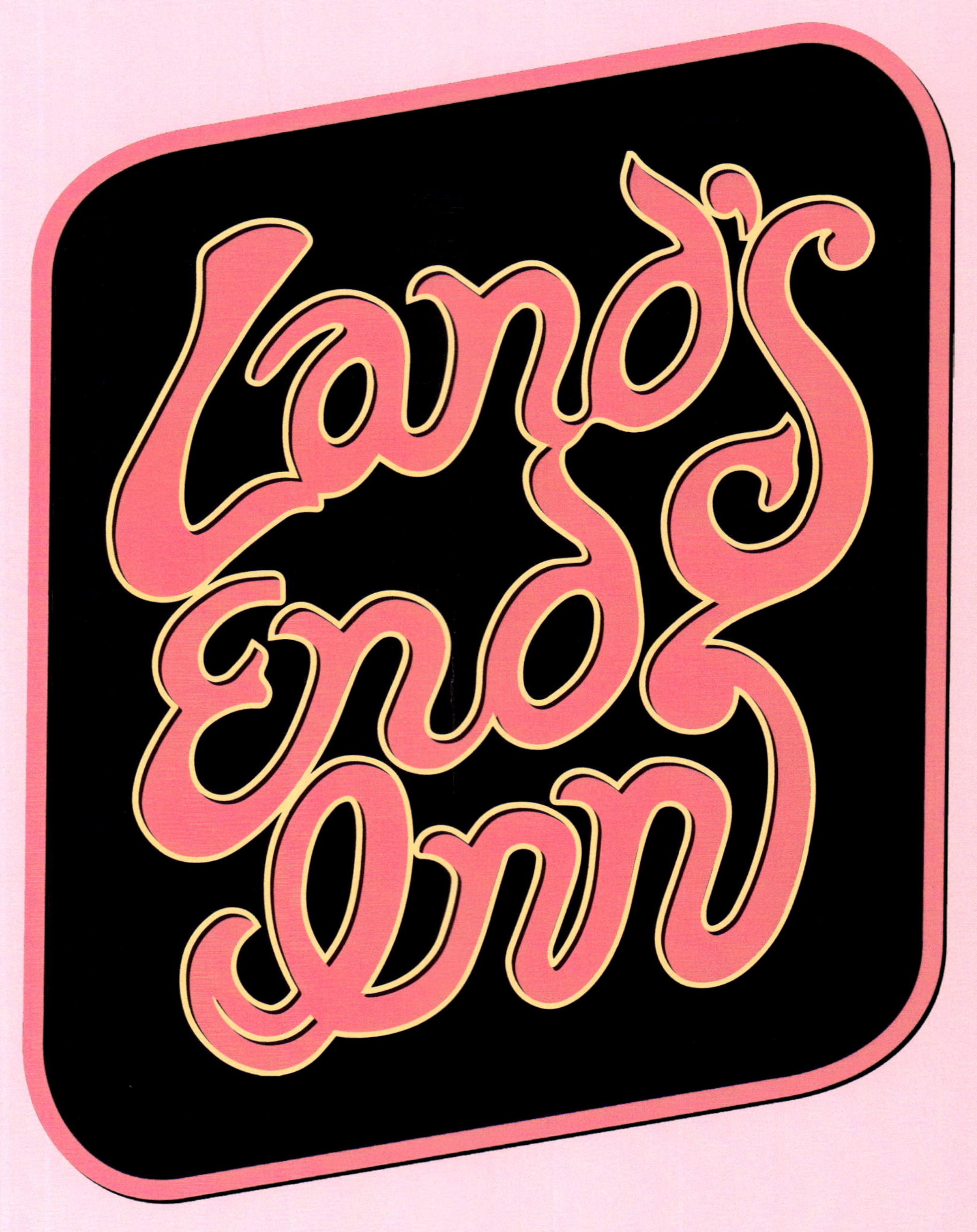

LandsEndInn.com